1

Drive

One Man's Road to Owning a Safari Business

By Greg Ward

Acknowledgments

There are many special people who made this book possible. First, my wife Debb and son Adam who provided support and encouragement throughout the project.

Of course, this book wouldn't have been possible without the graciousness and enthusiasm of new-found friends: Adam Stephen Meshallu and his parents Stephen and Dinnah, Zubeda Mukunde, Nandi O'dell, Steve Saxe and the many clients of Proud African Safaris who I interviewed along the way. Thanks to Lori Horth and Valeria Palmertree for their copy edits and to Julie Garel, fellow writer and creative inspiration. Special thanks to the hospitality of Arusha, including Arusha Serena Hotel and Lake Duluti Lodge. Book jacket design by Joanna Nuno.

ISBN: 9781795644976

CONTENTS

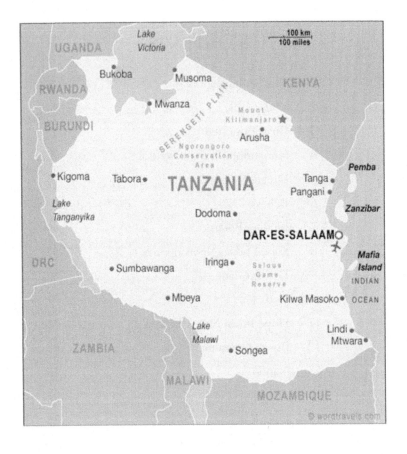

Chapter One

THE SERENGETI

"Let me know if you need to check a tire," our safari guide asked, as we jostled over dirt roads in Tanzania's northern Serengeti. "Road" is too kind of a description. With me were my wife Debb and our two close friends, Jamie and Todd – enjoying one of those bucket-list trips that seem to grow in number as you enter your mid 50s. We were traveling in an Army-green Land Rover over slivers of land with little or no vegetation but chock-full of potholes, divots and ruts. It felt more like driving across the back of a massive crocodile writhing from indigestion.

"Check a tire" is safari code-speak for alerting our guide that someone needs to exit the truck to use the bathroom. Toilet facilities were hard to come by. We were limited to *maybe* a couple of wilderness camps or a sketchy concrete structure disguised as a bathroom next to a dirt-packed runway some thirty bumpy miles away. When you have to go, you pretty much have to expose yourself to God and country and any creatures crouched in the nearby grass. It does make you think twice about going number one.

At 12,000 square miles, Serengeti National Park is about the size of Maryland. It aptly got its name from the Maasai word "Siringitu," which means "the place where the land moves on forever."

And that it does.

The landscape is pancake flat. Most of the park lies in Tanzania, but a thumb of it crosses over into Kenya to the North, where it's called the Masai Mari. The Serengeti is perhaps best known for The Great Migration during which some 750,000 zebras, 1.2 million wildebeest and hundreds of thousands of other animals make their annual trek around the Serengeti in search of lush grasslands upon which to feed. As result, thousands of predators feed upon them, creating the "circle of life" thing Elton John crooned about.

Our guide for this adventure into the Serengeti was forty-two-year-old Adam Stephen Meshallu, proud owner of Proud African Safaris, an Arusha, Tanzania-based safari guide service. He's strong and compact like a Division III football fullback. His waist-length dreads, often crammed under a mustard or Rastafarian-colored beanie, make him appear to be six inches taller than he actually is. He has a quiet laugh and an infectious smile, though I do wish he'd smile more. When chatting with him over a cup of coffee or in a safari truck in the African bush, he speaks softly, as if he doesn't want to scare any animals away.

"Adam, I need to check a tire," my wife, Debb, whispered. This trip was her idea, a result of her wanting to do something out of her comfort zone. I don't think she anticipated it would involve making comfort stops in the middle of Lord-knows-where – make that Lord-and-Adam-know where – here in the northern Serengeti.

As Debb got back in the truck after making sure "the tires were properly inflated," Adam politely asked, "Proceed?"

and with a collective, "Yes," we continued our game drive toward the Mara River, near the Kenyan border.

One of the big draws of a safari trip like ours — other than the opportunity to pee outside — is the chance to search for the coveted "Big Five," comprised of the African elephant, black rhinoceros, Cape Buffalo, lion, and the leopard. The "Big Five" designation was originally used by big game hunters to describe the most difficult animals to hunt on foot and was later adopted by non-gun-wielding tour operators as a way to market wildlife safaris. Adam told us, however, that in an effort to bring attention to smaller, less-noticed creatures of the savannah, there's now also the "little five," each sharing the first name of more sought-after Big Five. "There is the elephant shrew, the rhino beetle, the buffalo weaver (a bird), a leopard tortoise and the antlion." We wanted to see the Big Five, the Little Five and all the Fives in between.

To help, we brought along Zeiss binoculars, Canon and Nikon cameras and Todd's hefty black zoom lens, as big as my thigh, which we named "Jethro." Jethro allowed us to turn tiny specs in the distance into toothy predators up close and snap pictures that gave the illusion that we were much closer to the beasts than we really were. In many instances, however, the animals were almost close enough for us to pet, but such behavior is frowned upon — less you be munched upon.

The sheer number of animals we were surrounded by at times was mind-numbing. They dotted the landscape like manicured shrubs. It was soothing to watch them tend to calves, twitch a shoulder to shake off an insect, or quietly munch on a tuft of grass. There we were – clearly far removed physically and emotionally from our world of distractions, predictability and annoying headlines and deadlines – in this place, an ethereal place, savage but at times kind, a place of no rules and endless horizons, a place where one feels insignificant yet abundantly blessed.

It wasn't out of the ordinary to see thousands of zebra sauntering in a single file toward a mystery spot on the horizon or hundreds of pencil-thin Thompson Gazelles jittering about as if over-caffeinated, their small black tails swishing back and forth incessantly. By far, wildebeest were the most prominent species. They're an ugly lot — half horse, half goat, with a face only a mother could love. I wondered, if a calf were presented with mirror upon birth, would its immediate reaction be, "WTF?" But, it turns out, ugly wildebeests can make good friends, and in the easy-to-identify zebra they find a trusty traveling companion.

Adam explained that wildebeest are besties with zebra because, for starters, their striped friends are smarter. They have better memories for recalling past migratory routes and know which areas are safe and which are dangerous. In other words, wildebeest are not only homely, they aren't terribly bright. Adam explained that "wildebeests can be spooked by a predator, start to flee and in a matter of seconds, totally forget where they were running in the first place."

Intelligence aside, their eating habits complement one another's. Zebra have long front teeth, making it easier for them to munch on taller grasses, whereas the wildebeest graze primarily on shorter grass because their mouths are uniquely shaped in a way that makes feeding on roots easier for them. As a result, the zebra and wildebeest don't compete for food. That's probably enough on the unique relationship between the wildebeest and zebra, but it does help communicate an important point. With Adam as our guide, I learned more in ten days than I had in the past year. I now know the gestation period of female lions and can recreate the mating dance of male ostriches – if the mood is right. I know giraffes, although herbivores, gnaw on the bones of carcasses to get the phosphorous and calcium their bodies require. I learned cheetah moms chirp at their kittens rather than roar, or meow for that matter.

Regardless of the animal, whether it be the smallest insect, the most colorful bird, the most dangerous snake, or the most graceful cat, Adam possessed a deep knowledge about whatever it is we saw — or didn't see. On rare occasions, he'd refer to one of the many field guides he kept on the dashboard of the Land Rover, in the event that a random question should arise. For instance, our travel companion and part-time birder Jamie asked about the Latin name for the Secretary Bird – a rather tall, leggy creature that looks like it's wearing bike shorts and has haphazardly applied orange and red mascara. Black quill-like feathers explode from the backs of their heads. A few flips through a field guide and Adam told us it was Sagittarius Serpentarius.

Because we got to spend more than a week with Adam in the Serengeti, we learned that to be an extraordinary safari guide, it takes more than just book knowledge, the ability to locate elusive animals in the bush or the agility to safely ford a stream in a Land Cruiser. That's just the price of entry for carting around wide-eyed tourists decked in crisp, fresh-off-the-REI-rack safari clothing. Adam's goal for all the safaris he leads is for it to be the most memorable, can't-wait-to-post-on Instagram, make-your-neighbors-envious-at-cookouts kind of trip that's sure to be a truly life-changing experience. Adam confesses, "I just want to do the best for my clients. My goal every time I take them into the bush is to offer a unique, *fantastica* and amazing time no one else can offer. And I truly believe how I was raised, the people I met, and the things I went through to get where I am today is what makes Proud African Safaris special."

Chapter Two

THE CANDLE

Adam was born in 1973 and grew up in a small village about a twenty-minute walk from the town center of Arusha, Tanzania. Back then, when motorized transportation was a luxury, distances were calculated by how far it took to walk from one place to another. It bears mentioning that Adam is a Maasai, which threw me off at first because my knowledge of the Maasai — and it's embarrassing to admit — was limited to what I saw on the *Discovery Channel* or articles I read in *National Geographic*. I believed all Maasai men were tall and thin, that they always wore traditional red, plaid robes and sandals made from cow hides or repurposed motorcycle tires, and that they spent their days either tending cattle or competing in jumping dance rituals.

But there was Adam, a Maasai, sporting a khaki t-shirt with his company's logo and olive-green cargo pants, sitting behind the wheel of a late model Land Cruiser with a can of Pringles on the dashboard asking me questions about the current political climate in the United States. While the traditional Maasai lifestyle still exists in rural parts of Tanzania and Kenya, government intervention, climate change, population dynamics and exposure to other cultures — thanks to visiting tourists — have caused the number to decline over the years. But Adam's family's departure from the traditional

Maasai way of life began with the British occupation of Kenya in World War II.

At the start of the second World War, Kenya was still a British Colony, and as a result, many young men living in the country were "recruited" to fight Nazi oppression and protect British interests in East Africa. At the time, Kenya bordered Italian East Africa to the north, and it was feared that the much larger Italian army would advance into Kenya as it had in British Somaliland. Evidently, during the first half of the 20th Century, East Africa was ripe for harvesting able —but not too willing— bodies for military service to fight wars that had nothing to do with them.

"My father was in King African Rifle Army," Adam's father, Stephen, explained as we sat in two handmade wooden chairs on his porch in Arusha, sure to be the envy of HGTV fans back in the States. They were crafted out of tree limbs no thicker than a broom handle. The passage of time and visits from family and friends had sanded them down to the smoothness of polished marble. The limbs were woven in a way so the chairs were more than just comfortable. They felt like a hug from nature itself. Stephen and his wife Dinnah, whom he affectionately calls "Mama," live in a simple concrete home a mango's-throw away from Adam's house and on the same plot of land where he grew up.

The barrel-chested sixty-two-year-old Stephen wore dark short-shorts and a long-sleeved khaki shirt with sleeves rolled up to his elbows. A faded green, floppy safari hat and black plastic sandals rounded out his ensemble. He has an infectious energy and a permanent grin. When he speaks, his voice is deep and somewhat raspy. There was a staccato pattern to his detailed storytelling. His English was good, save for a few unique mispronunciations like "hopisital" (rather than "hospital") and "flow" (in lieu of "flour"). After making a point, he leaned forward slightly to encourage a response. Meanwhile, Dinnah sat quietly with her needlepoint and managed a smile an occasional nod as her husband explained his family's history to me.

Stephen's father, Melejacki Sindato, was captured by the British around the beginning of the Second World War. Stephen took a second and explained that Melejacki means "is always forward" and Sindato means "know how to sing for the ladies." Melejacki, along with nine other warriors, were in the bush celebrating the slaughter of cows, which was rare in Maasai culture. "They were in bush for two months, far away from women, having a feast eating meat and soup made from bark of trees. After they eat meat, they rest and started dancing. They see big truck coming. It was the British," Stephen explained. The warriors made a fateful decision and decided not to run because they didn't want to leave their food. According to Stephen, while they were watching the approaching truck, a small army of armed British soldiers and two black Kenyans appeared from behind, circled them and told them to drop their spears and knives and get in the truck. Melejacki didn't have the chance to say goodbye to his family. Young servant boys who were with them in the bush and not needed by the army managed to run back to the village and tell family members what had happened. "The people in village learned that when you see a truck, you know it's the army. You run away. Even cows run a way when they see truck," Stephen said with a laugh.

This wasn't the first time Adam's ancestors had run ins with European military forces in Kenya. His great-grandfather, Lomanyani Rugei, was kidnapped by the Germans in World War I and forced into hard labor for four months before escaping during a thunder storm, while the guard sought cover underneath a truck. Miraculously, he found his way back to his village more than 100 kilometers away to live happily with his ten wives.

"My father's experience with the British was much better than my grandfather's time with the Germans," Stephen explained. Melejacki and his fellow captors saw other Maasai warriors at the British camp who told them "there is no problem. There is no reason to worry. We are learning. We are in another school of the world." Stephen explained the British didn't shave his father's head with a broken bottle like the German's did with his grandfather. They did, however, lop off his hanging earlobes with a knife in an attempt to make them look like "normal ears."

Stephen said his father did make friends with the British in Kenya during his six years with them. "They taught him how to be a good soldier and leader. They showed him medicine for cows. And in the evenings, the soldiers taught him how to read and write English." By far, the most important, transformative thing the British did was introduce him to Christianity and the work of missionaries. Ultimately, he was baptized and changed his name from Melejacki Sindato to Alisha Lomanyani: "Alisha" after the prophet and wonder-worker of the Northern

Kingdom of Israel and "Lomanyani" out of respect for his father and in Maasai means, "one who is blessed."

"You know, missionaries? These people are like a candle. You know a candle?" Stephen adjusted his chair to face me directly and sat upright, shoulders back. Both hands were outstretched with palms up, as his delivery became sermon-like. "My father told me whenever they stay, they make a church. They make a 'hopisital' and then, school. So, it is a candle which is lighting the area. My father was explaining to the other Maasai, because whenever they see a white man, they run. So he was explaining these people are candles that light. Missionaries are not a war people. We are not in the war now. We are becoming Christians to change our lives."

When the war ended in 1945, the British treated their loyal recruits to a victory celebration, given a financial bonus and some much needed R&R. The British told Alisha to come back to Arusha in six months, in early 1946, and report to the district commissioner, where he'd receive a promotion and be assigned more military work. "The problem is once he got money, he changed his mind. He came back to his village. He sees his brothers and relatives, and because he has good money at the time, there is no need for more. It is better to marry. So, he marry my mother then," Stephen explained.

Money, the desire for start a family and good command of the English language weren't the only thing Elisha brought to his village. He became active with the Ilboro Lutheran Mission and was the first to introduce his family and other villages in and around Arusha, to Christianity. It was a transformative time for Adam's family, one that would change the way in which they approach life, relationships, childrearing and education.

Stephen said that both his father and grandfather were Stone-Age people, and he wasn't exaggerating. As Maasai, they were members of a nomadic tribe who lived in mud huts and relied strictly on animals for food, just like their forefathers before them had for thousands of years. Meat, blood and milk were the primary staples. The measure of a man's wealth was determined by the number of cattle and children he had. The "light" of Christianity changed all of that and more. It's safe to say that Alisha became the change agent for the family and for the broader community. For starters, he instituted nightly Bible study, morning prayer and a preaching method that can best be described as forceful persuasion.

"The light has started here. It is time to change from old Stone Age to a new generation," Stephen recalled his father saying. "It is now a shame to put on a Maasai blanket and carry a knife. It is better to wear a tie. Our life can be better than it is."

Stephen's father also separated his family from those who didn't want to change. He would take them to other villages, point out their poor living conditions and tell his family, "See this? They are living this way because they don't want to change. How can you see a book if there is no *light* here?"

Conversely, he took them to missionaries in and around Mt. Meru where there were new hospitals and modern schools with English-speaking teachers. He wanted to show them first-hand that these people were better off and more advanced because of the missionaries. "After I came back from there, I wanted to cry," Stephen said. "It really did make us think about our lives and what we could still obtain. We were following the root of our father. We wanted to work hard because he had shown us there is a difference."

While the acceptance and practice of Christianity provided a solid foundation for their family, it didn't hide the reality of Tanzania, which remained a difficult place to live and prosper. That holds true today and even more so when Adam was a youth. Hard work continued to rule the day. Their life was in a better place, spiritually, but some of their daily chores and –even some of their living conditions–were still reflective of the world of their Stone Age ancestors.

Chapter Three

BUSH EDUCATED

When Adam was between the ages of six and eight, he'd lie in his bed in the wee hours of the morning dreading the minute when his father's alarm clock would shrill, marking yet another day of nonstop chores. The family's two-room home featured a prized corrugated tin roof, dirt floors and mud walls that would crack in the dry season, allowing critters like lizards and bugs to slither about and interrupt his sleep. His mother patched the walls with a concoction of ash and cow dung. Often this did the trick, but the smoky-poop stench of this homemade spackle made him gag. He shared a room, a bed and a blanket with his younger brother, Christian, while his parents slept in another room where the darn alarm clock was.

When the alarm sounded at 5:30 a.m. sharp, Adam's father would roar a command in Swahili that loosely translates to, "Boys, time to get up. Grab something to eat and get started on your chores." Adam's morning routine would then begin. He'd put on a well-worn t-shirt, shorts and sandals and give Christian a nudge. "Christian, you'd better get up or father will come get you up!" Before chores, breakfast often consisted of a cup of goat's milk and a dollop of porridge served in bowls carved by his father. On some mornings, they had leftovers from the night before, which usually consisted of some greens and maybe some meat. Either way, what they ate in the morning had to sustain them until dinner that night. This was a tall order for growing boys with a full slate of daily chores of tending to goats, feeding cattle, gathering wood and the dreaded "fetching water."

"Fetching water was my least favorite chore," Adam confessed. "Walking to the water hole was the easy part; it was the walk back I didn't like." Typically, Adam and Christian would use three or four plastic buckets, but when those were filled to the brim, they had to stop every 100 hundred meters and rest. "Coming back took twice as long. I was convinced carrying those heavy buckets would give me the long arms of a monkey and a back as twisted as a vine." Days filled with nonstop chores were typical for most boys growing up in Tanzania at the time. Adam and Christian's role was to support the family and heed their parents' wishes. There was little time for play, and because Adam was the eldest child, the majority of the work fell on his shoulders. Literally. It would be another two years or so before he would start school, but until then, Adam said he was "primarily bush educated."

"Bush" is a generic term for any rural or undeveloped land of which Tanzania has an abundance. It's home to animals big and small, harmless and dangerous, beautiful and unearthly. It was Adam's backyard, playground, workplace and, more importantly, his first school. Nature was his teacher, and each day was a chance to learn something new.

Adam's family used a repurposed oil drum to store water, behind their home, tucked away in the bushes. When the water dropped to a certain level, he and his brother had to replenish the supply. One day, three other boys from his village — all of similar age and wiry stature —— had the same chore to perform. So, Adam and Christian gathered their plastic buckets, and the whole group set out about their day, probably looking like a ragtag drum corps of some lost marching band. The walk to the water source went through varying terrain– dusty fields punctuated by thick green vegetation consisting of elephant grasses, ground-hugging Congesta shrubs and prickly acacia trees that weren't shy about drawing blood.

Water sources aren't found in wide-open areas. Often, abundant vegetation is a sign of a possible water source. Knowing this, Adam and his water brigade made their way to a small ravine, the preferred water source for the past few months. They proceeded cautiously down a narrow path (because animals get thirsty, too), and suddenly, they heard something crash through the bushes. Whatever it was, it jumped. Wherever they were, they jumped. Buckets were tossed, and the boys darted toward an open area about fifty meters away. After they caught their breath and gathered their wits, they did the proverbial headcount to make sure everyone was safe.

And then, the debate began. "What do you think it was?" asked one of Adam's friends to which another chimed in, "It was leopard. Definitely, a leopard."

"It was much bigger than a leopard; I'm guessing it was an elephant," said another.

Adam laughed. "If it were an elephant, don't you think we would've seen something big? That's just crazy."

After a few minutes of this back and forth, they remembered that they still had to fetch water. Each of them knew far too well that their parents wouldn't accept an excuse about not bringing back water because they were afraid of an animal they didn't even see. They decided to walk to another water source a kilometer or two away. Evidently, the possible consequences of not completing their task outweighed the dread of a longer trek and the threat of hungry beasts, so off they went. The visit to the next water source was uneventful, the trek back, brutal, but Adam recalled the day's events as just another example of the schooling ways of the bush. "Perhaps the location, at that time of the day, wasn't the safest place to collect water. Maybe next time, we should be more aware of our surroundings when approaching the path. Maybe we should look for droppings or sniff the air to detect animals. Maybe we should talk less and listen more," he reflected.

Adam's bush schooling wasn't limited to just the wildlife areas in and around his home in Arusha. He made multiple trips to visit his aunt and her clan in the Ngorongoro Conservation Area, about a westward two-hour bus ride from Arusha. The conservation area itself is approximately the size of Yellowstone National Park and is home to the massive Ngorongoro crater, the largest unflooded and unbroken caldera in the world. It's technically a sinkhole rather than a crater and was caused when a volcano blew its top some three million years ago. It's estimated that before all hell broke loose here, the volcano would've been taller than nearby Mt. Kilimanjaro, which sits at 19,341 feet above sea level and is the tallest mountain in Africa. What's left now is a crater larger enough to hold the city of Boston with room to spare. And, if you plopped One World Trade Center smack down in the bottom, its top wouldn't exceed the walls of the caldera. It's a big hole in the ground and, surprisingly, a popular gathering spot for a variety of species.

Getting Adam to the Ngorongoro Conservation wasn't easy. His family didn't own a car. They saved money for a bus ticket from Arusha to a village called Karatu, over two hours away. From there, he'd a hop ride on a delivery van or safari truck to his final destination. His aunt lived in a traditional Maasai village in terms of its layout and adherence to traditional tribe practices. The clan lived in 10-20 kraals, or huts, arranged in circular fashion, all surrounded by a singular ring of stacked acacia thorns designed to protect cattle and villagers from pesky predators.

Adam's clan in the conservation area was made up of approximately 40-50 "members" and was a very efficient and productive community, due in part to clearly defined roles – a hallmark of Maasai culture. Women built and maintained the houses and collected firewood, raised children, milked the cattle and cooked for the family. Girls, too, helped with cooking and milking. Boys herded small livestock, fetched water and performed whatever other chores their fathers would assign. Warriors handled the community's security, and elders made political decisions and advised on day-to-day activities.

"It was much more primitive and traditional than my home in Arusha," Adam recalled. "It was very much an area full of wildlife, more so than Arusha. I saw zebras, hyenas, elephants and other animals there on a daily basis." But life for a young boy at his aunt's village still focused on work rather than play. There were always sticks to gather, water to fetch and livestock to care for. Being in this wilder environment helped Adam hone his skills in identifying the smells and sounds of potential predators. He became well versed in the various plant species in the bush and could predict the weather better than today's super Doppler radars.

"Great knowledge comes from growing up in the bush, being connected to the bush and loving the bush," Adam preached. "When I take clients on safari today, the kind of knowledge I gained growing up and experiences I had as a child, help me a great deal today. The more time you spend in the wild, the more confident and smarter you get. As I got older, I could identify animals by their smell even before I could see them. " I really don't think I could do those things if my childhood was different."

He also has this uncanny ability to spot and identify wildlife at great distances. While on safari with him, he directed our attention to a dark grey dot on the horizon, which turned out to be a male ostrich performing a mating dance. With the aid of binoculars and after a quick drive across a patch of savannah, we saw the ostrich in a crouched position, wings splayed. He was bobbing and weaving like a boxer. His long, thin pink neck was tucked back like he was trying to avoid punches – but was really trying to attract a mate. Thanks to the never-ending teachings found in the bush, even I can now identify the complex mating rituals of the male ostrich.

Adam's learning experiences from the bush provide a strong argument in the ongoing nature vs. nurture debate, with nature taking a slight edge in this case. That's not to say his parents didn't play an important role in shaping him into the successful businessman and likable person he is today. They knew the immense value of a good education, so they began home-schooling him around age five, providing him with a sizable head start to his formal education, which in 1970s Tanzania typically began when children reached nine years of age.

Chapter Four

KIMANDOLU PRIMARY SCHOOL

"See the blackboard?" Stephen asked, pointing toward a rectangular, black chalkboard the size of a welcome mat hanging on the shed next door, while we chatted on his front porch. "The first foundation of education starts with me and Mama. We had to make time to show them to love school and to learn. In the evenings, I would gather my children and teach them things like how to read clock, how to read and write Swahili and even some English. First, I started with how to hold chalk. You put it in your fingers like this," he noted, holding his left index finger as though it was a piece of chalk, while using his right hand to demonstrate the grip. "Then, I would use chalk and write 'BOMA,' which is Swahili word for where we keep cattle. That way they could see what 'BOMA' looked like when it's spelled out. Me and Mama know teaching them at home is a first step to make them love learning and to love school."

While similar types of scenarios have played out in homes throughout the world for countless years, Stephen explained his early attempts at teaching in a way that made it sound like this was one of the best ideas anyone had ever had. Like all parents, Stephen wanted desperately for his children to have a better life than he and "Mama." "We were there to plant the seed and help it grow."

When Adam turned nine, it was time to register for school. He and his father walked the three kilometers down dusty streets and through grassy fields to Kimandolu Primary school in Arusha. In the past, Adam had seen other students, dressed smartly in their school uniforms and matching book bags, make their way to and from Kimandolu. Now, it was his turn. Going to school not only meant learning so many new things; it was also an opportunity to "skip all the hard work at home," Adam said.

School registration in Arusha in the early 1980s differed greatly from how we register children in the States. For starters, the assistant headmaster asked young Adam to "take your right hand, lift it over your head and touch the top of your left ear." Feel free to try this at home. This rudimentary test was used primarily to gauge the approximate age of student applicants. If students could follow these simple instructions, school administration deemed them smart enough and old enough to begin school, which at the time, was anywhere between the ages of seven to nine. Another method the school used for assessing age was to have the students stand up against a wall where there was a height chart. If a student was roughly 127 centimeters tall (or four feet), odds were he or she was roughly eight years old. There was little to no record-keeping in Arusha then: no birth certificates to prove one's age, no baby books chronicling milestones in children's lives and no doctor's records. These two "tests" were the enrollment criteria at the time, and Adam passed them with ease.

DRIVE

These days, Arushan children start primary school at age five. A fortunate few attend preschool. Adam and I visited his primary school in the spring of 2017, his first trip back there in some forty years. A simply constructed and very wordy sign out front identified the school as "Ofisi Ya Rais Tamisemi Halmashauri Ya Jiji La Arusha Shule Ya Msingi Kimandolu" (Google translated into "Office Of President Regional Administration and Local Government, Arusha City Council, Primary School Kimandolu"), which makes for a rather wordy diploma or team name on a soccer jersey.

We drove onto the school grounds where we were met by a sea of green sweaters. Uniforms are the norm at both public and private schools in Arusha. Different schools don different colors and fashion combinations. For Kimandolu, the boys wear khaki pants and bright white collared shirts under a Kelly-green sweater. For the girls, it's Kelly-green calf-length skirts, white knee socks and, like the boys, bright white collared shirts beneath their sweater. Other area schools chose blue as their color of choice; for others it might be brown or grey. Regardless, the uniforms make for a handsomely dressed student body.

We parked out front where I quickly became the focus of attention. It's possible that I was the first white man in his 50s to visit the primary school in Kimandolu in a while – maybe the first ever. Every child was smiling, some waved excitedly and one even practiced his English on me. As I exited the truck, I dropped my pen on the ground, and it was quickly retrieved by a young boy who politely presented it back to me with a, "Here you go sir; you dropped your pen."

Adam and I made our way to the school's office in hopes of speaking with the headmaster. Just inside the main door, a few school girls were mopping the floors and cleaning the walls with threadbare rags – the price one pays for tardiness or not following school rules, Adam explained. The headmaster was out, but we did manage to speak to the assistant headmaster, a who was more than happy to show us around.

The school had grown considerably since Adam had attended, with its current enrollment now hovering between 600-700 students. The campus consisted of an administrative building and a long row of 10-12 dimly lit classrooms housed in a solidly built concrete block structure. Each classroom was slightly larger than a two-car garage and contained a slew of small, well-worn wooden benches and desks facing a large black chalkboard practically covering the entire wall. Colorful posters attempted to hide the grime on the remaining walls. The back windows overlooked the grassless, sloping soccer pitch, while the front classroom door opened up to a dirt courtyard landscaped with a few scraggly shrubs and bowling ball-sized stones painted white.

Adam pointed out his first-grade classroom; in typically Western tourist fashion, I poked my head through the doorway, where I startled a teacher reading aloud to previously attentive students. Out in the courtyard, students acted like students. A group of boys demonstrated their soccer dribbling skills while shouting either Swahili words of encouragement or universal sport "trash talk;" I'll never know. Clusters of girls chatted, pointed and giggled. Teachers were never far away.

The scene here was no different from the school yards of Atlanta or Chicago.

While we walked around the school grounds, Adam explained how his informal home schooling proved beneficial as early as the first grade. "Because I knew basic reading and writing skills when I started school, I assisted my first grade teacher, Ms. Mollel, with simple tasks like showing other students how to hold a piece a chalk and teaching them the Swahili alphabet." Back then, these eight - and nine-year-old students were beginning what we'd in the states refer to as the first grade without the benefit of any prior formal school experience. There was no pre-school or kindergarten, but that's the way the Arushan school system operated. Children were crucial members of the family's workforce and were needed at home to perform important chores in their early lives.

Adam attended primary school at Kimandolu for seven years, the customary time before moving on to secondary school. During the first two years, he learned the basics of reading and writing — all in Swahili — as well as arithmetic. During year three, he started to learn English, although he knew some already, thanks to his parents. The classes he took in grades four and five foreshadowed his future; it was then that he was introduced to the sciences and to history.

"Two books really influenced me," he explained to me. "There was this book about the digestive system with colorful illustrations about how food and nutrients work their way through the body. I was fascinated immediately. The other book was called *All the Stone Age*. Many fossils and stone tools were discovered right here in Tanzania. Oldupai Gorge in the

Rift Valley, which is an important archeological site for human evolution, is only four hours from here." This is where in 1959 British/Kenyan paleoanthropologist/archeologist royalty Mary and Louis Leakey discovered fossilized parts of a skull and upper teeth of a type of hominin not previously identified. They dated the discovery as having lived 1.75 million years ago, making it the oldest hominin discovered to that point.

Chapter Five

DREAM CHASER

Adam excelled in primary school. His interest in nature and the sciences continued into secondary school, where he took classes in agriculture, math, science, biology and physics.

"I didn't plan to become a safari guide," Adam confessed. "I had different dreams and aspirations. My plan was to become a doctor, a children's doctor. " Curiosity was the driving force in this pursuit, and one of the largest science labs in the world was right outside his door. Procreation, birth, growth and death were topics to be researched and further understood. "I loved observing and studying baby animals because they provided true information on how life starts from stage one after birth to adult age. I pictured myself studying and specializing in helping kids be healthy and grow."

It was Dr. Urasa who played an important role in helping fuel Adam's interest in the medical field. He remembers Dr. Urasa as a tall, slender man with snowy white hair and thin rimmed glasses, who possessed a charming personality and a bedside manner that was the envy of other physicians. He was a family friend who just happened to operate the Old Arusha Clinic not far from where Adam attended secondary school. Dr. Urasa immediately took fifteen-year old Adam under his wing. Right away, he made sure Adam had face time with the other doctors practicing there. He arranged lunch meetings between them, offered Adam a private area in which to study the hospital's medical books and encouraged him to experience first-hand what it was like to be a doctor in Arusha. Two weeks later, Adam attended his first surgery, the removal of a goiter from woman's neck.

"There I was fifteen years old, dressed in surgical scrubs and walking through these double doors into the operating theater," Adam shared with pride. "I was able to peek over the surgeon's shoulder during the operation. Then, I witnessed an operation to remove these growths from a man's shoulder and then a highly-invasive stomach surgery." Surprisingly, Adam didn't get queasy and credits his many hours poring over countless medical books featuring detailed, colorful drawings of various parts of the human anatomy. He quickly became a familiar fixture around the clinic, dropping by after school, during school breaks and holidays or whenever he could muster some free time.

A humble Adam said ,"The way the whole hospital community was so helpful and friendly and how they encouraged me on a daily basis to pursue my passion sealed the deal for me for wanting to become a doctor." Throughout secondary school, he pursued this dream in the classroom and in frequent visits to the clinic.

Upon completion of secondary school at the age of seventeen, Adam had his sights set on attending Machame Medical School in the Kilimanjaro region, east of Arusha, which now goes by the name of the Machame Health Training Institute. His grades were exceptional. He had practically interned at Arusha Hospital. And his mentor, Dr. Ursa, was a key member of the medical college, so Adam was confident that his application would be accepted. However, one significant, and unfortunately, impossible obstacle stood in Adam's way: lack of money. At the time, tuition for one semester at Mechame cost about $250 USD. Adam's family barely made ends meet as small-scale dairy farmers. They had four other children to raise, his brother Christian and sisters, Endesh and Leah. Student loans were rare, and the ones available were almost impossible to secure.

One afternoon, Adam and his father sat in front of the family's home and had what one would call a heated conversation about possible next steps. His father suggested a variety of options: "Adam, why don't you go to secondary school for two more years?" Your uncle is a chief general in the Tanzanian army; why don't you enlist?" "Maybe you can learn a trade and become an electrician?" Adam, being a stubborn and driven seventeen-year-old, shot down all suggestions that were hurled his way.

His head and his heart were so focused on becoming a doctor, he wasn't interested in any options that didn't have something to do with science or medicine. Unfortunately, the reality of his situation became very clear, and Adam surmised that if becoming a doctor was going to be virtually impossible, it was time to think of a plan B.

Chapter Six

BELIEVE

Adam spent the next six months in a funk. His dream of becoming a doctor quickly and painfully faded. His father continued to suggest random career choices, all of which Adam rebuffed. Desperately aware that he needed to find something else to do and devote his time to, he sought consolation in his stack of school textbooks and the books he got from hospital staff. His interest in the sciences remained strong, so he read and reread many of these books and made repeated trips to the regional library to peruse books about nature, biology, anatomy, history, and wildlife. It was there that he re-discovered his creative side and spent hours drawing and painting recreations of the illustrations in his books: pictures of wildfowl, mountain ranges, tree leaves, and body parts. Although school was over, Adam feverishly continued his personal studies, feeding his mind with the subject matter that made him feel most alive.

His personal development was also hugely impacted by music, which Adam saw as "another teacher for me. You learn from music 'life is a struggle;' things aren't always going to be easy, but we can overcome it." Adam found comfort and inspiration in Bob Marley's classic Reggae hit "Three Little

Birds." Perhaps it's a bit predictable but very appropriate considering the challenges he faced.

Rise up this mornin'
Smile with the risin' sun
Three little birds
Pitch by my doorstep
Singin' sweet songs
Of melodies pure and true
Saying', (this is my message to you)

Singing' don't worry 'bout a thing
'Cause every little thing gonna be alright
Singing' don't worry (don't worry) 'bout a thing
'Cause every little thing gonna be alright

In addition to popular reggae music, Adam also found encouraging messages in the Christian-based songs performed by a central-Tanzanian group called Nkinga Christian Choir. Curious, I pulled up a few of their videos on YouTube, and, while the production quality leaves something to be desired, the performers do sing and dance with evident passion. After listening to eight to ten of their songs, it's evident that a synthesizer, bass guitar and drum machine are the instruments of choice. At times, the lead vocals are cringe-worthy, but the backup singers make up for it with delightful harmonies and rhythmic swaying.

One of Adam's favorite songs by the Nkinga Christian Choir is titled *Mpende Mungu Wako (Love Your God)*. A few of the verses, all sung in in Swahili translates loosely to, "When you are patient and stand on the right path, pray to God. Search... believe you will be successful." Adam definitely took these words to heart. While his original chosen path was medicine, he remained patient, prayed and knew in his heart that he'd be successful in whatever career path he chose. "Believe it or not, I never got discouraged. Frustrated, yes but never discouraged," Adam told me.

One afternoon, while walking in Arusha, he was reminded of how fragile life can be. He ran into a former classmate named Absolon who had fallen victim to drugs. Adam recalled that in grades three and four, Absolon was a good student and a trusted friend. But during secondary school, his demeanor changed. He struggled with school and was no longer the carefree and cheerful friend Adam remembered. "I ran into him downtown shortly after we finished secondary school. I thought it was odd he didn't recognize me because we'd known each other practically all of our lives. When he spoke, he sounded very confused and rambled on about things I didn't understand. When you see something like that, you get scared. And he wasn't the only one of my friends who lost their way. It's easy for it to happen here. So, I made it a priority of mine to stay positive, make sound decisions and follow the right path no matter what."

Because of Arusha's close proximity to the Serengeti, Ngorongoro Conservation Area and other natural areas, park rangers were a common fixture for Adam – which gave him an idea. Why not become a park ranger? It was in line with his passion for the sciences and nature – and likely didn't come with the hefty price tag of medical school. He replaced his medical books with more wildlife books and began researching options around Arusha to help him achieve his "Plan B." He soon discovered that The College of African Wildlife Management was located near the village of Mweka on the southern slopes of Mt. Kilimanjaro, approximately 100 kilometers from Arusha. Today, it's a well-respected and award-winning institution responsible for training over 5,000 wildlife managers from 52 countries worldwide since its inception in 1963. In addition, he discovered the TANAPA (short for Tanzania National Parks) ministry office was located right in Arusha. This office is currently charged with managing all sixteen of Tanzania's national parks, from the well-known Serengeti National Park and Mt. Kilimanjaro National Park to the lesser-known Saadani and Ruaha national parks.

With this newfound intel and uncurbed confidence, Adam walked an hour to get to the TANAPA ministry office headquarters, showing up at their door step unannounced. He was seventeen-years-old and as fearless as a lion. "Security out front stopped me right away when I said I wanted to speak with the Tanzania National Park General," Adam recalls jokingly. In the U.S., this would be equivalent to a recent high school graduate just showing up in Washington, D.C., requesting a one-on-one with the Secretary of the Interior. While Adam was unable to sit down with the General himself, he did sweet-talk his way past security and met with a few of his assistants. "You never know 'til you ask," Adam beamed.

Adam explained his new career goal and peppered them with questions about the preferred work experience, educational requirements and job duties of national park employees. He also asked if they would be open to the idea of sponsoring him for additional education. He proposed TANAPA could help with tuition costs at The College of African Wildlife Management. In return, he would work for the ministry office after school at little or no pay with the mutual agreement that he'd have a job upon graduation. This sounded good in theory, but Adam soon learned that typically, it's the college or institutions, rather than the Park Ministry, who sponsor the students.

Never one to get discouraged, Adam saved up the bus fare and traveled two hours to The College of African Wildlife Management. Not having learned his lesson from his unannounced visit to TANAPA, he showed up at the college with lots of excitement – and no appointment. Fortunately, this time he wasn't stopped by security but rather met with an admissions counselor, who gave Adam an overview of available courses in conservation, tourism administration, biology, and wildlife law-enforcement, all of which interested Adam greatly. "Just hearing him describe the classes and the learning environment reassured me I was making the right decision; I really wanted to engage myself in the wildlife field." However, while the tuition was considerably cheaper than medical school, his family still didn't have the financial means to pay for advanced education.

Adam was now desperate for a job. Any job. This was the second time in under a year that the hefty college price tag stood in the way of achieving his goal. Finding employment in Arusha in the 1980s wasn't easy. Unemployment was, and continues to be, a significant problem there. Cracking open the Sunday paper and scouring through the wanted ads wasn't an option. Adam had to get creative. As luck would have it, he found helpful job contacts in cattle dung, of all things.

Chapter Seven

FINDING FOCUS

When Adam was young, his parents were small scale dairy farmers. They started out with two cows, Saba Saba and Kadogo. Over time, the heard grew to over thirty cattle and Adam's father used to deliver milk in canisters tied to the back of his Raleigh bicycle. Back then, he could get upwards to 800 Tanzanian Shillings per liter, which wasn't much but every little bit helped a growing family with ambitious dreams.

Around the time of Adam's job search, domestic bio gas was introduced to Tanzania. In its simplest terms, bio gas production removes gas from waste (in this case, cattle dung), turning it into an energy source used for powering lights and also suitable for cooking. Adam's father met two German entrepreneurs named Christopher Klinger and Alex Schlusser through a mutual friend. Klinger and Schlusser worked closely with Adam's father to set up a small scale bio gas operation on the family's property. The successful plant became a local model for domestic bio gas production and as a result, people from throughout Africa and as far away as Frankfurt, Wales, London, and Munich made the trek to Adam's home to learn more about the operation.

Proud that his home was now a scientific attraction of sorts, Adam's father started keeping visitor books chockfull of details about everyone who toured the property. Those books still sit on a shelf at his home in Arusha, along with family photos and knickknacks. Time and hungry insects have taken their toll on at least one of the books. The baby-blue cover was stained by the many hands who've flipped through its pages. On the cover, "Stephen Elisha Meshallu" was written in dark blue ink in all capital letters, in such a way that the "allu" portion became jumbled and notably smaller as it crowded its way into the cover's right-hand side. Insects seemingly munched away at the bottom left-hand corner, exposing the interior pages, creating what looked like the outline of a snowcapped mountain on the background of a baby-blue, murky sky. The pages were organized with column headings (date, name, address, occupation, and signature) in both English and Swahili, and were primarily lined in blue ink, with a smattering of entries in black and red.

Annika Wager, a veterinary student from Manchester, England visited on July 7, 1987. A journalist from Nairobi with dreadful handwriting dropped in earlier in the month. Robin Teater from Seattle, Washington, and Robert L. Lauren from Greenville, West Virginia were there two years later. Each book contained roughly 150-200 names. When Adam was in his teens, he greeted these visitors from far and wide and assisted his father in giving tours of the bio gas plant. "I showed them around and explained the container domes, the piping and the process," Adam recalls. "It was fascinating to speak to people from all of Africa and different parts of the world. There were environmentalists, scientists, college professors, and even the president of Tanzania came by one afternoon."

The professionals listed in his father's visitor books became Adam's contact list for job search and tuition assistance leads. He went through each book page by page and identified the people with whom he spoke personally and started what he called his letter-writing campaign. "I wish it was as simple as it is today, shooting a mass email to all those people. It wasn't. I must've handwritten over 100 letters." He persuaded his father to give him some money to purchase stamps and would mail a small batch of letters at a time. Then, he'd write a few more letters, bug his father for more stamp money and mail some more. This went on for months. A few responded with a pleasant note. Most didn't respond at all.

Finally, Adam got a hit. The wife of Dr. Sarone Ole Sena of World Vision Africa offered him a job as a gardener. World Vision is a Christian relief, development and advocacy organization dedicated to working with children, families and communities to overcome poverty and injustice. While touring the bio gas plant, Dr. Ole Sena was impressed with the grounds and gardens around Adam's family home, so he suggested to his wife that they hire him to maintain the landscape for their property as well. As an added incentive, Adam was offered full access to their personal library so he could continue his self-study. Armed with enthusiasm and garden tools, Adam went to the Ole Sena home every day for two weeks straight and transformed their property into a garden oasis. It became the envy of their friends and led to more gardening work. Although the pay was minimal, Adam slowly contributed to his growing college savings. "I realized this was just a step in the process I had to take. For me to pursue a goal, I knew I needed money to fund my studies. I picked up a shovel and got to work."

Despite his hard work over six months, Adam still didn't have anywhere near enough money to enroll at the well-respected College of African Wildlife Management. At the current rate, it would take years before he could attend. He pleaded his case to his father, and they arrived at a plan that they were both happy with. Instead of applying to the wildlife management college, he would start taking classes at Mount Meru Tour Guide School with some financial assistance from his father. This school operated much like community colleges in the States, meaning that Adam didn't have to foot the bill for an entire semester but rather, could pick and choose classes based on his interests and the amount of money he had at the time.

Mount Meru Tour Guide School was founded by a gentleman, Horace Nsari, whose mission was to provide further education to prospective students who couldn't afford to attend larger, more traditional schools. Mr. Nsari had been a teacher at The College of Wildlife Management for twenty years and adapted syllabi to fit students interested in being naturalists, tour guides, or involved in other areas of the growing tourism economy. In his first year, Adam took classes in hospitality management, botany and mammal behavior. He'd run out of money and go back to gardening or pouring drinks at a local bar (another skill he picked up along the way) until he saved enough money to take more classes. "After the first four months or so, I thought less about becoming a park ranger and more about becoming an ambassador for the country and for the guests who are traveling here," Adam contemplated. "I saw the role tourism played in our country and the money it brought in. People had jobs because of it."

With that perspective, Adam narrowed his career focus to becoming a safari guide, blending his interest in the sciences and wildlife, his knowledge of the bush and his desire to educate guests who visited Tanzania and the nearby parks. He started a list of area safari companies to apply to by simply jotting down the company names he saw on the many safari trucks that transported visitors around Arusha. His initial list included companies like Ranger Safaris, Abercrombie and Kent, Simba Safaris, Fly Catcher Safaris (what an unappealing and pesky name) and Tropical Trails. He began cold-calling these companies, and in true Adam fashion, he just showed up unannounced. Tropical Trails was one of the first places he visited.

Surprisingly, Tropical Trails was in desperate need of guides, and they interviewed Adam right there on the spot. They were very impressed with his academic record and coursework in tourism. They loved that he was fluent in English and were impressed with his thorough knowledge of wildlife and the surrounding parks. As a result, they invited him back the next day to take a driver's test.

"That was a big problem," Adam shared with a smile. "I'd never been behind the wheel of a car, ever. I left the interview and told them I would see them tomorrow at 1 p.m. for the test, but I had all kinds of thoughts racing in my mind: 'I am so close to getting a job. My heart is asking me what are you going to do? This is something I can't fake! How could you not know you needed to know how to drive?'" He waited outside of the building, mentally kicking himself, until he saw the woman with whom he had interviewed exit the building. He approached her and admitted that he didn't know how to drive and apologized for wasting their time. Her reply was quick and painful: "This job was yours."

Adam learned from that experience. He had to. To get a job as a driver guide, he needed to know the job requirements inside and out. He conducted informational interviews with a few more safari companies, and common job qualifications became apparent: For starters, applicants needed a good academic performance in wildlife studies. He had that, so, check. You had to be a very good driver with no tickets. No check for the good driver part, but a check for no tickets. You needed at least three years' work experience. Half a check, maybe. You needed a driver's license valid for more than three years. No semblance of a check, whatsoever. And, being fluent in not only English, but also French, Italian or German was a plus. Check for English. No check on additional language skills.

For Adam, this growing list of job requirements meant two things: more time and more money. He figured it could take anywhere from nine months to two years to learn the basics of a new language and roughly three years to secure a valid driver's license. The driver's license requirement in and of itself was a huge roadblock (pun intended), seeing he didn't know the difference between a carburetor and a camshaft. As for work experience, he faired a little better with stints as a gardener, bartender, and even as a substitute Sunday school teacher. He couldn't accomplish any of the above without more money, so he relied on his contact list again. After more misses than hits, he discovered that a friend of his father's was in management at a hotel property called Sopa Lodge at Ngorongoro Crater (yes, the same Ngorongoro Crater). Adam's timing couldn't have been better. The lodge was preparing for another hospitality training program for interested and qualified candidates. A quick introduction to the right person at the right time, and Adam was off to Sopa Lodge.

Chapter Eight

SOPA LODGE, NGORONGORO

Sopa Lodge Ngorongoro is a ninety-seven-room lodge catering to tourists on safari in Ngorongoro Crater and surrounding parks like Serengeti National Park to the West and Lake Manyara and Tarangire to the East. The lodge sits at the highest point on the crater's rim and offers exceptional views across this enormous caldera. Because it faces west, guests are drawn to its patio at the end of the day to watch the brilliant African sunset. Chairs on the back porch are coveted and often occupied more than an hour before nature's evening show begins. Wildlife on the floor of the crater are not visible from this vantage point, but you can watch shadows from passing clouds migrate across the landscape, creating a mélange of dark greens, deep blues and bright yellows. When the sun sets, guests don't applaud in Key West fashion but rather sit quietly, mesmerized by the changing colors and how the last vestiges of light inch behind the crater's rim once again.

Adam began his three-month training making a paltry $5 month, $1.50 of which was deducted as a breakage fee, as management assumed trainees were going to break something. However, meals were included, as was a uniform and a place to stay. Adam shared a small bunk room with other trainees. Days were long and stressful. There was so much to learn about so many departments. While the payment arrangement was borderline criminal, Adam saw the training program as an opportunity to get more work experience with the hopes of being hired full-time, at which point the pay would be better.

"I wore this name tag that said 'Adam – Trainee,' which was a long way from having a name tag I hoped one day would say 'Dr. Adam Meshallu,'" Adam said with a hint of regret. "But there I was at Sopa, and I was determined to make the most of it." The training program involved rotating through the lodge's various departments, including kitchen, restaurant, front desk, laundry, housekeeping, public areas, and the bar/restaurant. For Adam, the toughest parts were the kitchen and restaurant training because it involved many words with which he wasn't familiar.

"What is this thing called coriander soup? What is a coriander anyway?" "Have you had this soup before?" Adam quizzed me one afternoon. "The other departments were much better. "He seemed to excel in those positions in which he interacted with guests. During his training, Adam couldn't help but notice that there were always safari trucks parked out front, which made him jealous. There he was reading clothing tags in a windowless, muggy laundry room, making sure he didn't add bleach to this load vs. that load, while driver guides were out searching for elusive Black Rhinos and lion cubs. He continued to remind himself that eventually his day would come.

After three months of training and impressing managers in every department, Adam earned a job as a bartender at Sopa Lodge. Although he was more interested in working at the front desk, bartending did provide an added incentive: guests tipped for good service, especially after they had a few drinks. This gave Adam an idea.

A co-worker of his made weekly trips to the nearby village of Karatu to pick up lodge supplies. One day, Adam approached him and asked if he needed any help making the supply run. "I really wanted to go along so I could ask him to teach me how to drive. I was willing to give him some of my tip money in exchange for lessons," Adam recalled. Initially, his friend was reluctant. Using a company-owned vehicle for personal use was grounds for dismissal. Adam eventually persuaded his friend by suggesting they pick a spot many miles from the lodge to avoid being caught.

"Mentally, I was very prepared to drive. I had ridden in cars and trucks many, many times, but driving was not easy as I thought it'd be," Adam admitted. Steering, while shifting gears, checking the mirrors, monitoring speed, and keeping and an eye on the road, presented a bit of a challenge. "I spent a lot of time in gears one and two on those roads. Getting into higher gears meant going faster, which I was not ready for." Adam's driving lessons continued off and on for a few months, until he was confident enough to apply for a driver's license back in Arusha.

Just to be safe and to ensure he'd encounter no problems with obtaining a license, Adam convinced his father to pay for classes at Mamrose driving school, which, funny enough, had a curriculum more intensive that than of the States'. Instruction lasted two hours every day (with the exception of weekends) for an entire month and involved thirty minutes of classroom time, during which Adam learned about traffic signs and rules of the road, followed by one and half hours of behind-the-wheel instruction.

In Arusha, it's evident that the vast majority of drivers didn't attend this driving school, or any driving school for that matter. They tend to make up their own rules by disregarding stop signs, going off-road should they encounter one of the ubiquitous traffic jams, and trying to break the world record for the most people in a mini-van. Honking appears to be the second language of motorists, with the first being Swahili, accompanied by creative hand gestures. Encountering traffic police is as rare as seeing a black rhino in the bush. If you do happen to see them, they tend to travel in pairs and are dressed in crisp white uniforms like U.S. Navy officers heading to a fancy dinner.

After completing driving school, Adam went to the police station, passed the driver's test and was presented with a driver's license. While this was, of course, a crucial step in becoming a guide, most of the safari companies still required guides to have a valid drivers' license for at least three years. He told his father about this, resulting in yet another driver's test.

"My father said, 'go find a car and put me in it and let's go for a drive,'" Adam explained, hinting this had likely been the hardest driver's test thus far. "We drove to town and back in an old, black 505 Peugeot." Adam's father didn't have a lot to say during the drive. He just peered out the window and watched cars and motorcycles stir up clouds of dust on Arusha's bustling streets, occasionally commenting on their peculiar driving habits, like how they disregarded road signs and came dangerously close to hitting a pedestrian or two. When they got back home, his father merely said, "I'll work on it." After a week or two — a period during which Adam's father talked to a friend of a friend who knew a guy who had a boss — Adam driver's license went from being valid for two weeks to being valid for three years. "My father never wanted us to take shortcuts in life. He always instilled in us the value of hard work. So, it was out of character for him to help make my license older than it really was. It showed he supported my goals," Adam said.

Adam with a client planning the next day's game drive.

Wildebeest and Zebra brave the Masai Mara in the Serengeti.

Elephants slowly make their way across the savannah.

A lioness and her cubs start the day off with a morning drink while
keeping an eye out for safari trucks.

Adam's parents, Steven and Dinnah, with family photos in front of their home in Arusha. Steven is currently a safari guide in Tanzania like his son.

Adam picking up clients at Kilimanjaro Airport, Arusha

Adam's grandfather, Melejacki Sindato, was captured by the British in Kenya during WWII and became a member of the King African Rifle Army. During this time, he was introduced to Christianity and later shared his faith with family far and wide.

Adam, in foreground, helping his family with chores.

Students between classes at Primary School Kimandolu where Adam
attended as a youth.

A Maasai village outside of Serengeti National Park has
become a popular tourist stop for safari guests.

Zubeda Mekunde, Proud African Safari's operations manager and co-founder of Skilled Hands Tanzania which helps young women learn a marketable trade.

A cheetah keeps an eye out for her cubs in the Southern Serengeti.

Adam's wife, Caroline and daughter Nandi, sharing a cup of tea outside their home in Arusha.

Morning views from a tented safari camp in the northern Serengeti.

It's estimated that over 250,000 zebra roam the Serengeti, but the wildebeest population here exceeds two million.

Arusha market is a place of sensory overload where sights, sounds and smells collide.

Wildebeest jockey for position during a treacherous river crossing.
Photo by Todd Fifield.

Impalas are fantastic jumpers. They can leap as far as 33 feet (10 meters) and as high as 10 feet (3 meters), according to *National Geographic*. Photo by Todd Fifield

Cat nap. Photo by Todd Fifield.

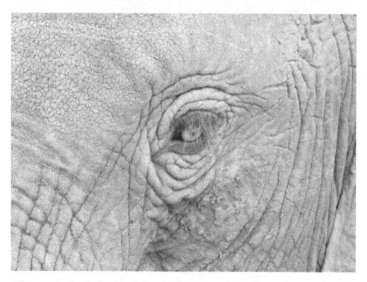

The cracks in their skin help elephants retain moisture between mud
baths. Photo by Todd Fifield.

Chapter Nine

DRIVER GUIDE

Eventually, Adam left Sopa and returned to Arusha to continue looking for employment opportunities with safari operators. In his mind, he wasn't getting any younger. At age twenty-three, Adam was eager to pursue his new career choice. Having this new driver's license and four years of hospitality experience under his belt gave him a renewed level of confidence; yet he had one last hurdle to overcome. Once again, he relied on his contacts.

One of his primary school classmates, a girl named Omega Oningo, taught Swahili to English and Americans working in Arusha. Omega shared an office with young German woman by the name of Ms. Potzdam. Like Omega, Ms. Potzdam taught Swahili but to German workers. Omega invited Adam over to their offices to meet this kind German lady, and she agreed to teach him German in the evenings for the next eight months. Recognizing his passion for learning and his previous success at "self-learning," she gave him stacks of German language books, which he took home and pored over religiously.

"I knew this was one of the missing pieces in achieving my goal. I wasn't going to let learning another language get in my way. The language has similarities with English, but it was still difficult," Adam said. At night in his parents' home, he'd borrow the family radio and take it to his room. There, he'd put it on the bed next to him and slowly turn the dial until he found the Deutsche Welle station, which still catered to Germans living in East Africa.

Along with learning German, Adam saved up enough money working at Sopa to pay for another six months of classes at Mount Meru Tour Guide School. There, he took additional classes in wildlife management, geology and guiding. Being back in Arusha was a wise choice. He could continue his studies where most of the safari guide companies were located. After all, "you can't find a job when you're living in the bush. I needed to be back where the businesses were and where the outfitters were located." His days were jam-packed. He attended classes at the wildlife college in the morning, followed by one-on-one instruction in German. Afternoons were devoted to job-searching.

Adam encountered what appeared to be a new wrinkle in becoming a safari guide. Most of the driver guides were older than Adam, mainly in their thirties and forties. Some were even older. Interview after interview, prospective employers told him flat-out that they weren't comfortable or confident in sending a "young boy" to guide tours anywhere, let alone the Serengeti. "They saw me as just a kid," Adam said with frustration. "They were afraid how I would respond to solving client problems and whether I was old enough to lead groups. This was very difficult to hear. Now, age was getting in the way of becoming a guide? What is next?" Adam sought guidance of a member of the family clan, an elder named Leaky who guided with Ranger Safaris, a well-respected company based in Arusha operating tours throughout Tanzania and Uganda. The elder did what was commonly known as a "hard sell" to management about Adam, and they granted him an interview within the week. Adam clearly recalled that the first interview with them went really well. They asked basic questions about his work experience, knowledge of wildlife, formal education and his experience growing up in the bush. A second interview focused on problem-solving and language skills (primarily English), with just a few questions relating to conversational German.

Last was the all-important driving test. "I really wouldn't call it a driving test; it was more like a quiz. They would call out part of the safari truck, and I'd have to point it out to them. It was strange. Antenna. Wheel spinner. Lift jack. Spare tire. CB Radio. Now, turn on the radio. Now, turn off the radio. Open the bonnet. It was not what I was expecting." The closest thing to testing his skill behind the wheel was when the interviewee told him to drive the truck across the dirt parking lot. "I climbed in the truck, put it in first and slowly drove across the lot. It wasn't more than 25 meters. No turns. No stops. Just straight. Of course, I passed" Adam boasted.

Finally, Adam became a bona fide safari guide in 1997 with Ranger Safaris, making 50,000 Tanzanian Shillings a month. While that's roughly $25-$30 USD a month, it was still five to six times more than what he had made as a trainee back at Sopa.

Unbeknownst to Adam, his first assignment was back at Sopa Ngorongoro Lodge, taking clients down into the crater.

At the time, Ranger Safaris sent a lot of business to Sopa Lodge, and they needed guides on site to lead tours. On his first evening there, he visited with some of his former co-workers and later made his way to the housing units reserved for guides. It was a small bunk room with a narrow, uncomfortable cot, side table and a small storage space for his gear. There, he met his fellow —and significantly older— roommates Yusuph and Nixon. Burly men with short, cropped hair and bloodshot eyes. Few words were exchanged, likely because competition was fierce among drivers, even among drivers working for the same company, and even more so, among the competition. And this still holds true today.

The next morning, Adam met his very first safari clients in the lobby of the Sopa Lodge, a family of five consisting of a couple in their late-forties and their three teenage children. Adam admitted he was a little nervous at first, especially when the father introduced himself and his family in very broken English, made more unintelligible by a thick French accent. One of the teenage girls inserted herself in the conversation speaking in English he could better understand. The group chatted for a few minutes about the day's plans, and Adam was careful to speak slowly so that they could understand him. They piled in an ARQ 336 Land Rover TDI, turned right out of the lodge complex and shortly began their descent into the crater.

The dirt road leading into the crater was barely a truck's-width wide and strewn with rocks, some as big as softballs, which Adam navigated with ease. Switchbacks were common, wildlife less so. They tend to hang out in the flat landscape of the crater floor near water and food sources. Roads are still dirt here, but are flat and easy to navigate. There are few trees on the crater floor, making for prime wildlife-viewing. Wildebeest cross roads as if safari trucks were invisible. Zebra congregate in groups called a dazzle. When one yaps at another, which sounds oddly similar to a hyperactive Chihuahua at the back door, the dazzle disintegrates. Birds flitter. Warthogs look mean, ornery and downright silly. Short muscular legs support a plump body and a huge head. They're slightly larger than their distant cousins, the barnyard pig. Two pair of fleshy wart-like clumps — hence its name — and two pair of fierce looking tusks compete for its most prominent facial feature. They boast little fur except for a thin, dark mane down the center of their backs. Their tails are whip like and stick straight up like car antennas when they scurry about. Adam pronounces these homely critters, "war-THOGS."

During this first safari, Adam treated his clients to all this and more, including quietly watching a pride of lion relax in the grass and even saw an elusive black rhino rubbing its signature horn on a yellow acacia bush. Day one as a guide had certainly been a success and long overdue for Adam.

As the sun set over the crater, Adam reflected on not only recent events but also on the long, often circuitous journey that led him to his current position as a safari guide. Not becoming a doctor no longer haunted him. He found a new passion, one that capitalized on his experience growing up in the bush and his deep love for nature. As an added bonus, he had really enjoyed spending time with the French family despite the minor language barrier. "It was like a cultural exchange," Adam recalled. I learned about their life in France, and I told them about my life in Africa. It was very special."

For the next three years, Adam took clients in and out of the crater: Americans, English, Canadians and, yes, even quite a few Germans, allowing him to showcase his basic German skills. Most months, he guided 17-20 trips into the crater. There were a few months where not a day went by that he didn't guide. He'd wake up, get dressed, eat a quick breakfast, do maintenance on the truck, grab the boxed lunches for his clients, meet them in the lobby, drive to the crater in search of animals of varying shapes and sizes, and then drive back out. During those rare occasions of free time, he went to his aunt's village for a home-cooked meal or went to Karatu, the closest major village to the lodge, to pick up supplies.

Karatu is a bustling outpost an hour southeast of Sopa Lodge Ngorongoro. Like many villages in Tanzania, clay red is the dominant color. Dust covers the road, buildings, push carts, and the people pushing push carts. The road, sometimes splattered with white bird droppings, runs smack down the middle of town. Adjacent to the road, people sell things, fix things and wait for things. Colorful vegetable stands are tended to by middle-aged women wearing bright dresses and even brighter smiles. Teenage boys are eager to sell you beads, bracelets, shoes, or canned soda. Younger women walk about with baskets, bundles or bowls on their heads filled with fruit, stacked clothing and who knows what else – their cargo held firm by years of practice and strategically tied colorful heard scarfs. A few carry precious cargo on their backs, babies with smooth bald heads and curious eyes. Young men wait patiently on less than reliable dirt bikes ready to offer rides to locals and adventurous tourists who don't realize the importance of wearing helmets — Karatu's version of Uber X.

For Adam, it was a slice of Arusha away from the predictability of life at the lodge, where his days were planned in detail. One of his favorite restaurants was Vijana Junction, which offered vegetarian options, great service and a homey atmosphere. A waitress named Caroline Melkiady caught his eye one day and would later steal his heart, eventually blessing him with a son and daughter. Caroline has a bright smile and a soft-spoken demeanor.

I shared a cup of homemade mchaichai tea with her, Adam and three-year old daughter Nandi one spring morning under the shade of mango and eucalyptus trees. Adam set up a card table and chairs on their lawn, while Nandi stood close to her mom, a little unsure about her parents' guest for this impromptu tea party. While Caroline's English is limited, she has a way of communicating with her eyes and gentile smile. When she speaks, it's in a cautious whisper, as she carefully selects words from her limited English vocabulary. When asked a question she doesn't understand, she nods apologetically and turns to Adam for a quick translation to Swahili. Adam said her smile, honesty and work ethic were the things he admired most when they first met.

Caroline had to work hard to keep a smile on her face when she first met Adam because her four younger siblings, ranging in ages from six to sixteen, depended on her emotionally and financially. Caroline's mother passed away when she was seventeen, and her father left the family two years prior. She "celebrated" her eighteenth birthday as a mother, father, provider, life coach, and a proverbial shoulder to cry on for her younger brothers and sisters. To pay the bills and put food on the table, she got a back-breaking and thankless part-time job at a coffee farm harvesting beans, where she was paid based on how many buckets she filled. It didn't take long for Caroline to realize that being paid the equivalent of twelve cents per twenty-liter bucket filled was not going to be anywhere near enough to take care of her brothers and sisters. The most she could fill in a day was about five to seven buckets. After two months, her older sister, who sold vegetables in the Karatu market, told her Vijana Junction was looking for a waitress. She applied, got the job and could now better provide for her family. Plus, she enjoyed waiting on people, rather than being weighed down with buckets of coffee beans.

She was reluctant to talk to me about her first impressions. Shyness and lack of confidence in speaking English, the likely culprits. After waiting on Adam at the restaurant a few times, he began to request her by name. "I really admired how she put family first and filled in to be the parents for her brothers and sisters," Adam said. "Plus, she was very beautiful, but she sure did play hard to get."

While their relationship flourished, Adam became increasingly frustrated with Ranger Safaris and guiding solely in Ngorongoro Crater. While he always receiving glowing reviews from clients, it appeared to Adam that Ranger Safaris didn't want to mess with a good thing. Going in and out of the crater, over and over again was starting to wear on Adam. "I was desperate to take clients to other wildlife areas, like Tangarie, Serengeti and Lake Manyara, but they wanted to keep me just at Ngorongoro. I wanted to do more and be more than what I was."

Adam refused to be pigeon-holed as just a driver guide in Ngorongoro crater for the next 30 years. He had the drive to be more, learn more, contribute more and do more. In December 2000, after three years, Adam left Ranger Safaris. With Caroline now in tow, he quickly got a job with Bush Back Safaris Limited in Arusha. They lived in a tiny 6' x 15' wooden house with concrete floors on his parent's property. One interior door led to a simple sleeping area barely large enough for a bed. The kitchen and outhouse were out back. Two years after moving in, they welcomed a son, Steven.

Now with Bush Back Safaris, Adam was finally able to take clients to different ecosystems, but once again, he encountered what appeared to be an ongoing practice in the safari business: Do what you are told and don't rock the boat. "I lasted five years there, much longer than I really wanted to. They put you in a box and use you. They don't care if you want new opportunities, like furthering your studies or becoming a better person, as long as you are just making the current clients happy and nothing more." His next move would be to another safari company where he hoped things would get better. Unfortunately, things got worse, but eventually – and finally – things got better for Adam.

Chapter Ten

ZUBEDA

There is a Swahili proverb ("chovya yamaliza buyu la asali") that means "constant dipping will empty a gourd of honey." Adam's past experiences with various safari companies began to take a toll on him. It became more evident he would be happiest by becoming his own boss and being in control of his own destiny. While Adam quickly realized his new employer was no different from the ones prior, there was a bright spark in Adam's new company: a sweet soul with a heart of saint former classmate from his days at Mount Meru Tourism college named Zubeda Mukunde.

Zubeda has a melodic tone to her voice. At times, her accent is thick, but overall her English is wonderful. Occasionally, "Rs" replace "Ls" so "college" becomes "correge" and "knowledge" becomes "knowridge." At thirty-seven, she speaks with the confidence of a seasoned business woman but can also be motherly and passionate when talking with new friends or old acquaintances. Most of the time, she's dressed to the nines in colorful African garb made on her own sewing machine. Other times, she wears a Proud African Safari t-shirt with pride because she's been the operations manager at PAS since its inception back in 2009.

Zubeda's story is interesting in and of itself and perhaps deserves its own book. Her parents were refugees of the Rwanda Revolution in the late 1950s and early 1960s. They were one of over 300,000 Tutsi's (the second largest ethnic population in Rwanda) displaced by the Hutu (the country's largest ethnic population) during three years of ethnic conflict. They ultimately settled just over the border in the Kagera district of Tanzania, where Zubeda was born in 1980. There, her parents eked out a living as small-scale farmers, and the family grew to include twelve children. "My parents wished to go back to their honey and milk country, as they call it." Zubeda said to me. They wouldn't return to their native country until just after the Rwandan Genocide in 1994, when over 800,000 Rwandans were killed over the span of 100 days.

Rather than return to Rwanda with her parents, Zubeda chose to move south to the village of Mwanza to live with her sister when she was fifteen. "My father was not happy. I was his only baby remaining at home with them, as all my other siblings had left home to look for life, and my other sisters had been married off. On the other side, my mom had a feeling I was going to be somebody in this life because I was very bright in school, and she never wished for me to be married off at a young age." In many cultures in Tanzania, girls are considered ready for marriage when they reach puberty, an effort to protect them from premarital sex and pregnancy. Traditional customs at the time, and still common today outside of urban areas of Tanzania, called for marriages to be arranged by the parents of the bride and groom, in which a dowry or bride price is negotiated. Often this took the form of livestock, clothing or other items offered by the groom's family in exchange for the daughter's hand in marriage.

After about a year in Mwanza, Zubeda made her way to Nairobi, Kenya to be with yet another sister in hopes of advancing her education. In 1995, the school system in Nairobi was different than it was in Tanzania. Most fifteen-year-olds in Nairobi were finishing up high school and technically, Zubeda was a middle schooler at best, according to the school's standards.

"The schools weren't accepting me because one, I can't speak the language, 'Engrish.' So, then I started going to the baby classes, where I learned to say 'stand up, sit down, hello.' I repeat everything the teacher says with the kids half my age," she recalled. She kept looking for other schools, and with the help of her older sister, they found a school accepting students — only Muslim students — many of whom where refugees from Somalia and Ethiopia. The only problem was that Zubeda was not Muslim. She was actually born a Christian on Easter, and her birth name was Epiphania Emmanuel. In order to enroll in this school, she posed as a Muslim, changed her name to Zubeda, donned at hijab and started classes again. She chose the name Zubeda because she had a classmate of the same name back in Kagera.

After graduating in 2001, she bounced back and forth between Mwanza and Nairobi working as a seamstress, a secretary, and an English translator, earning money to take computer classes so she could be more marketable. She got married, had a son and soon thereafter, her husband died of blood cancer. After a year or two, she became bored with secretarial and administrative work and turned her sites on a job in the growing tourism industry, eventually taking classes at Mount Meru Tourism College, where she would eventually meet Adam. Coincidently, the first tourism job she landed was being a "meet-and-greet person" for the same company where Adam worked. Her primary responsibility was self-explanatory: She met and greeted safari clients at the airport, helped transport them to hotels in Arusha prior to trips to the bush, and then escorted them back to the airport at the end of their adventure. But unbeknownst to management, Zubeda added looking out for the well-being of the driver guides to her list of job responsibilities.

She professed "driver guides can make or break a safari company. They are the front-line workers for the business. They spend more time with the clients than anyone. Good service means more referrals. And, if you a sell a good itinerary to a client but do not present your guides at the best level, then they will not present anything that is good for the company." Although she'd only been employed with them for a few weeks, she understood the basics of how good customer service was paramount for business growth and employee development.

One of the interesting dynamics in her role as a meet-and-greet representative was it put her in a position to speak candidly with safari clients as she transported them back to the hotel or airport post-safari. Because she knew the importance of customer service, she'd ask clients very pointed questions about the safari, the guides, the accommodations, and the other tour offerings so she could provide management with recommendations on how best to grow their business. These interviews also gave her a clear picture of the performance levels of all twenty or so guides currently employed there. She knew the top performers from the underachievers. "Being on a safari is a time where your clients should learn and be inspired. Those drivers who are like teachers and quickly become your friend are the best kind of guides, not the ones who sit behind the wheel and just drive you to the bush and back." Zubeda said. Adam was consistently ranked in the top five, often holding the number-one spot for long periods of time based on client reviews and feedback from various tour operators. He was the type of driver guide who made safari owners a tad nervous, because he put the clients first and always had the ambition to be the best in his field. At times, Zubeda noticed some drivers who were getting the best comments from past clients were being passed over for safaris by drivers who historically didn't perform well. "Why would you not want to provide the best to your clients?" said a frustrated Zubeda.

It turns out it's about control, because frankly, driver guides own the client relationship once their guests hop into the safari truck, and that makes their bosses nervous. Management of these companies want their guides to be really good – but not too good. They want skilled and personable guides so they get positive online reviews, testimonials and more importantly, referrals. If clients have an exceptional experience with a driver guide, they'll likely refer friends and family and tell them to *specifically* request a particular guide. And, if that same client wants to return for their second or third safari, they'll likely request the same guide because they know their experience will be exceptional again. This is great repeat business and an obvious revenue generator for the company – but what happens when exceptional driver guides start working for another safari company? Given the choice, clients will always choose having the same guide over using the same safari company.

And therein lies the rub. To the best of my knowledge, non-compete clauses are rare in the safari guide business. And in this age of emails and social media, it's easy for driver guides to maintain contact with past clients. Many companies prohibit or frown upon the exchanging of contact information between driver guides and clients, because it literally puts guides in the driver's seat for maintaining the relationship and potentially taking future business with them. If safari companies can "control" their guides – for instance, by preventing them from pursuing additional educational opportunities and maintaining relationships with clients "post-safari" – then there's a stronger likelihood for future business/revenue through an already established channel.

Many guides are perfectly okay with this arrangement. They're thankful to be employed and perhaps are not as hungry to advance themselves. But Adam is an exception. He works tirelessly to achieve his goals. Along the way, he's persevered. When one door closed, he broke a window. He stayed positive despite obstacles. And he found strength and support from family and friends – and from a past client from New England.

Chapter Eleven

HOPE FROM NEW ENGLAND

There's no such thing as a jet bridge at Kilimanjaro International Airport (JRO). Upon landing, travelers exit either from the rear or from the front, depending on their seat assignment. It's quite an efficient way to deplane. It's a short walk across the tarmac to a terminal resembling an elementary school from the 1960s. A wide sidewalk flanked by attractive landscaping leads to a one-story, brown concrete brick building where passengers enter a cue with luggage and passports in hand, and a strange mixture of anxiety and excitement begins making its way throughout the rest of their bodies. This is, of course, the dark continent — full of mystery, hungry predators and a lifestyle foreign to visitors who are used to safe and predictable things like Grande lattes and reliable cell phone signals. The name "Kilimanjaro International Airport" in large U-Haul orange letters stretches practically the entire length of the terminal.

Steve Saxe, a New England-born, bred and educated businessman, along with his wife and friend landed at JRO for the first time in January of 2008 for a twelve-day southern Serengeti safari. They had hopes of seeing the biannual great migration in the Ndutu area just north of the Ngorongoro Conservation Area. Fifty-eight-year-old Steve trained to be an attorney but chose to manage the real estate portion of his

Massachusetts-based and family-owned retail company, instead. He's business savvy, business-driven and a do-gooder who cares considerably for the well-being of other people, wildlife, and the environment.

An avid traveler and nature lover, Steve said "I've always been intrigued by Africa but never had an interest in going." He has a noticeable Boston accent, and his stories are either very descriptive or consist of short and to-the-point sentences. Both are often punctuated with laughter. He's definitely a "Boston guy" with all of the grit, comedy, and sarcasm that comes with it. "The interesting thing is my wife kept sayin' 'I want to go on an African safari.' I want to go on an African safari' so I says okay; I'll find someone to take us on an African safari." He did what most people did then — and still do today— and researched online and found a U.S.-based tour operator specializing in private safari tours in Tanzania. He liked what he saw and booked the trip months in advance.

"You know, like everyone does, the first trip you go on, you gotta book way in advance. It's so far away. It's a big trip. You know, whatever, it's monumental. You're going from Boston to Kilimanjaro on the other side of the planet. Looking back, now it's a nothing trip in the grand scheme of things because I've done it so many times." But the first time did take its toll on him.

For the novice traveler, Tanzania isn't the easiest place to get to from the States. Steve's travel party began their trip with a six-hour KLM flight from Boston with a two-hour layover in Amsterdam, followed by an eight-and-a-half-hour flight to Tanzania. Jet-lagged from overnight travel and the seven-hour time difference, they deplaned a few hours after sunset and were met by warm breezes and an enthusiastic representative from the safari company named Zubeda. After customs forms were filled out and luggage was collected, they piled into an awaiting van and were transported to Arumeru River Lodge forty minutes away.

Ground transportation at night in Arusha is interesting. For one thing, it's dark — really dark — once you leave the airport. Dust and smoke loiter alongside the road, concealing darkly clothed people making their daily commute on foot, on bike, or on motorcycle. Drivers pass when the mood strikes, rather than waiting their turn for traffic to subside. On the way to Arusha, you drive through pockets of civilization with colorful and hard-to-pronounce names like Maji ya chai, Kikatiti, and Sing'isi. There's often a party-like atmosphere where people mingle, haggle over prices at food stands, or pass the time watching cars play chicken from the comfort of plastic lawn chairs.

"The first couple of days were a blur," Steve recalled. "I believe we rested at the lodge, went to town, but we were really looking forward to heading to the bush to start our safari." The most efficient way to get to the Serengeti from Arusha is to hop on a bush plane from the much smaller Arusha airport fifteen minutes west of town. Bush planes seat about nine passengers, provide half the headroom of a minivan and travel no more than twice as fast. Here, small prop planes ferry brave tourists to and from the Serengeti, Dar es Salaam and Zanzibar. Steve's destination was Seronera Airstrip in the northern Serengeti, not too far from the Kenyan border. It's called an airstrip rather than an airport for a reason. The word "airport" typically denotes forced smiles from gate attendants, beeping carts, bitching passengers, security pat downs, taxis stands and the ubiquitous Starbucks. "Airstrip" means a hard-packed dirt and grass runway that reminds you of a grossly unattended golf fairway. Bathing hippos, the water hazard. After a bumpy landing, a handful of green extended cab Land Rovers wait for planes to birth luggage and tourists covered in dust, awe and sweat.

This is where Steve first met Adam, his safari guide and future business partner. "One of the things I liked about him was he hit it off with my wife right away. She was a little apprehensive about being in Africa, but there was something about him that made her — and us —feel very comfortable and at ease." Some of Adam's past clients have also described him as genteel. He is polite, soft-spoken and professional. After a few minutes of light-hearted banter, he'll crack a smile laugh, quietly, and then quickly give you a "man, you're crazy," look.

Steve's travel party spent the next twelve days with Adam, chasing the migration, sneaking up on resting lions, getting dizzy from looking at the converging lines of zebra stripes, and learning more about nature and wildlife in Africa than they could have ever imagined. Steve had always been interested in wildlife conservation, even counting Osprey on a regular basis with the Marblehead Conservancy south of Salem, Massachusetts. He bonded with Adam over this interest in conserving all things wild and wonderful. Steve admitted to having started making plans to visit the following year even before this inaugural trip ended. "Adam and I never discussed anything business-related on this trip. It was all about making our trip memorable. He loves sharing his country with others, respects nature and its wildlife. We quickly became friends, and I was looking forward to coming back," said Steve.

After this trip was over, Steve and Adam stayed in contact through emails and social media, as friends do, but as safari guide "protocol" prohibits. Steve learned more about Adam's past, and Adam learned more about Steve's. As time went on, Adam shared his frustrations of working for other safari companies: how they often don't encourage personal growth of driver guides, how some guides go so far as to bribe management for bookings, and how some guides are simply blacklisted from future bookings for minor offenses. Steve relied on his business experience and offered words of encouragement, but it wasn't until he started to book his next safari that he realized the challenges Adam faced.

In the fall of 2008, Steve was finalizing plans for a second safari trip for the coming January. Around then, Adam was completing two months of classes at Limpopo Field Guiding Academy in South Africa, which was paid for by one of Adam's past clients but not fully supported by his current employer. "They were not a big fan of me going to South Africa. I think they punished me when I returned by not giving me any trips, even though I always got great reviews. I was no longer in the top pool of drivers," said Adam. "All I wanted to do was learn new skills and then take those skills into the bush and provide better service to their clients." Not being in the top pool of drivers is one thing, but his current employer took it one step further and temporarily "hid" Adam from Steve, who had specifically requested him for an upcoming trip. After a few heated phone conversations with management, Adam was assigned to be Steve's driver guide for a trip in January 2009. But still, all this drama prompted Adam to give serious consideration to branching out on his own. He just didn't know how.

"My past experiences working for other safari companies and the most recent one where I believed I was punished for going to school motivated me to think about starting my own company. I shared my dream with Zubeda, and she quickly started to do the math. 'How are you going to do all this without money?' Zubeda asked me. 'Listen Adam, you are just earning 8,000 Tz shillings a month ($50USD). How are you going to buy a truck or start you own business? They have been keeping you in the garage and you're not going on safari. You aren't even getting any tip money. How are you going to do this? Who is going to give you this money?'"

Chapter Twelve

BUSINESS REALITIES

There are more than 200 Safari Companies in Arusha – some big, some small, some new, some old, some reputable, others not so much – and they all share two common challenges: access to capital and customers based on a different continent. After a quick peek on the internet, I located a slightly used four-wheel-drive Toyota Land Cruiser with an extended cab and one of those nifty pop-top roofs allowing for a 360-degree unobstructed view of wildlife for just under $100,000 USD – quite a hefty price tag, especially considering the average monthly household income in Arusha is about $100, if you're very fortunate. To put things in perspective, if you have no other expenses and are able to save $100 a month, a slightly used Land Cruiser will be yours in a mere 83 years.

Local banks provide even greater hurdles according to an Arushan entrepreneur who wished to remain anonymous. "There's certain level of discrimination in the banking and lending institutions in Tanzania," he said softly, as we met over a cup of tea at a busy cafe in downtown Arusha. Before making a point, he always looked both ways and leaned forward. It was if he was afraid someone was eavesdropping on our controversial discussion. The sounds of the city at times drowned out his explanations, so he often had to repeat himself. "We discriminate amongst ourselves. If I go to the bank with you — and *even* if you don't have a sound business idea — you will likely get the money from them that I won't get in my own country. It's a pity. I may go there with a very good business idea; but I will not get the money here at home. We don't have that trust in each other. It is very difficult for small business to access capital."

In Tanzania, most small businesses or aspiring entrepreneurs also don't own assets worth enough in the bank's eyes to be pledged as collateral. For those few who own property, banks still might not consider that as secured collateral because owners historically have had challenges in proving legal and enforceable title to land. What's more, if applicants can't provide documentation showing salaried employment, an existing bank savings account, or demonstrate they truly can make weekly payments, they'll likely be declined. Adding further insult to injury, loans tend to be limited in amount, have no grace period, are short term and carry exorbitantly high interest rates often hovering at around 14-16% to upwards of 20%.

This is one of the reasons why foreign investment or partnerships tend to be the preferred route of choice for many wanting to start a business. Let's face it, more developed countries have a greater percentage of residents with money to invest and who are altruistic, like Steve. "I didn't go into this thinking I was going to make a lot of money; my calling was to help make a better life for them and their families."

Foreign investment/ownership also helps with the other major challenge of starting and running a successful safari business: 99% of the time, the target audience for those interested in safari trips live thousands of miles away, often in Europe, Canada, Australia and the United States. Having a basis of operation for marketing and accounting where your audience lives is simply smart business. Many people outside Africa are simply afraid to send money to an entity in a strange country, let alone Africa, thanks in part to the slew of so-called "Nigerian" email scams — one of the latest hoping to raise $3 million to get a Nigerian man back home from his secret space mission. Having the money go through a reputable American bank makes safari clients more comfortable and provides an extra sense of security. Also, being in a similar time zone as your customers makes it easier to have phone calls about booking and itinerary options. Lastly, the knowledge base and resources for key marketing initiatives like public relations, web development, and media strategy are stronger than in Tanzania.

Chapter Thirteen

NANDI

2008 was an important year for Adam. He realized that, if he was truly going to be an exceptional driver guide, he needed to be in charge of his own destiny – maybe even own his own company – one day. In 2008, he met Steve. He also met a woman named Nandi O'Dell from Columbus, Ohio. It just so happens that 2008 was also an important year for Nandi, who made three life-changing decisions that year: She and her husband Mason decided to start a family, she left the 70+-hour work week world of advertising, and she convinced her city-slicker husband (her words, not mine) to go on Safari in the Serengeti. She managed to squeeze in running a marathon, as well.

"I always wanted to go on African safari, but I realized if I was going to do that, we needed to go before we had kids because it'll probably be a lifetime, 18 years or so, before we could do it again," Nandi confessed to me. Although this was going to be her first time going to Africa, she developed an early interest in the continent's culture and wildlife thanks to her professional ice hockey-playing father.

Her father, Robert Braden Houston and his wife Judith, who goes by "Chipper" lived in Johannesburg, South Africa in the mid-1960s before Nandi was born. Here, Braden played professional ice hockey of all things, while his wife worked for Kenyon Advertising. Surprisingly, the International Hockey Federation has 21 member countries across the African continent, with teams in Egypt, Morocco, Kenya, Zimbabwe and South Africa, to name a few. While there, Braden and Chipper befriended an anthropologist in Johannesburg who was studying the Zulu tribe. You may heard of Shaka Zulu, perhaps the most influential monarch of the Zulu Kingdom, from a 1980s television series about him. Well, Shaka's mother's name was Nandi.

"Nandi, means 'the sweet one' but actually she was quite wicked, so the story goes," Nandi said. This Nandi is all sweet, no wicked. She's the type of person you'd want as a next-door neighbor, one who'd volunteer to pick up your kids up at hockey practice, or bring a bottle of wine, along with great stories, to a cookout. Her shoulder-length auburn hair and Crest toothpaste model smile are her most striking features. She chooses words effortlessly without an "um" or "ah" getting ever in the way of her talking about her kids, her African Safari or her first introduction to the dark continent some thirty plus years ago.

"I grew up in a home where there was a zebra skin rug and sable antelope horns on the wall, along with African masks and artwork. I remember my parents used to put on slideshows for their friends about their experiences, which definitely sparked my interest in Africa and wildlife." It wasn't until the spring of 2008, that Nandi and her husband made it to Africa and went on safari. Coincidently, they used the same company

Steve did, even though it would be months before they would meet.

"When we descended into JRO in the pitch-black night sky, I saw this one tiny glowing orange light down below, which I later learned was a campfire in a small village. I thought to myself, 'where in the world are we?'" Nandi recalled. "But when we deplaned, I remember being hit by the heat, hearing these loud chirping bugs, and smelling smoke from distant fires and thinking to myself, 'I'm definitely in Africa.'"

As was the case with Steve's visit, Zubeda was there to meet and greet them. She helped them navigate through customs, gather their luggage and walked them out to the parking lot, where Adam was waiting next to his safari truck. "I thought it was the coolest thing being picked up in an actual safari truck by this guy with dreads down his back. That drove home for me what an exciting and unique experience this was going to be. During the trip to the lodge, Nandi thought Adam seemed shy, almost nervous, maybe even too serious. But Adam understood his clients traveled thousands of miles and spent thousands of dollars to come to a strange and perhaps scary place for a likely once-in-a-lifetime safari trip. A lot can go wrong. His job is to make sure nothing does.

After a day of rest, Nandi and husband Mason hopped on a bush plane at Arusha Airport and flew to the Grumeti airstrip in the western corridor of the Serengeti. The great migration passes through here between May and July, as hundreds of thousands of zebras, wildebeest and tagalong gazelles and antelope make their way to fertile lands into the north as they have for thousands of years. To get there, herds must first cross the Grumeti River, which hugs the northern border of the western corridor. As a result, the river becomes one of the most popular dining spots for great Nile crocodiles this time of year. These toothy creatures sometimes grow to the length of 16 feet and patrol the river like U-boats, waiting for the right time to strike, drown and then eat animals who dare to cross.

"I remember flying over the Grumeti on the approach and looking down and seeing the crocodiles and huge hippos in the river. There we these giant marabou storks with six-foot wing spans making them look like pterodactyls. I really felt like I'd been transported back into prehistoric times," Nandi said. "It's very intense if you haven't seen or experienced anything like that before. I felt like I was brought into a whole new world." And waiting at the airstrip to share his world with these somewhat intrepid travelers was Adam who had driven up from Arusha.

Nandi remembers the safari began the moment they loaded their bags into the safari truck. Adam is constantly on the outlook for wildlife big and small. If he could, I'm sure he'd love to be able to rotate his head 360 degrees so he wouldn't miss the slightest shake in a bush, flap of a wing, twitch of an ear, or track in the mud.

"Look, they are hunting," Nandi recalled Adam saying shortly after he picked them up from the airstrip, his truck now stopped near the Grumeti. Nandi, hoping to see a pride of lions or a cackle of hyenas so soon, looked from side to side with her camera at the ready. "No look, down," she remembered Adam saying. He had pointed out a line of army ants marching across the road. It wasn't the great migration Nandi expected, but it did demonstrate Adam's love for nature and his uncanny eyesight.

Adam is excited to bring people into his world and introduce them to incredible wildlife, regardless of how big or small. Each creature plays an important role in the Serengeti's fragile ecosystem, and Adam often teaches this during his safaris. It's that "circle of life" thing again. As the days went on for Nandi and Mason, the wildlife got bigger and the experiences more memorable. Adam led them to elephants, Cape Buffalos, hippos, lions, and giraffes, all the while providing valuable nuggets of information about eating habits, gestation periods, migratory patterns, family dynamics and who usually eats whom. Adam also told them stories about how elephants can be very aggressive, how the cape buffalo was one of the most menacing animals in all of Africa, and how hippos kill more humans every year than any other mammal. According to data compiled by Mother Nature Network, each year, approximately 3,000 people succumb to hippo-related deaths. Mosquitoes deliver the deadliest and most incapacitating punch, with mosquito-born illnesses killing upwards of 750,000 people a year according to the World Health Organization. "All this danger, danger, danger talk didn't sit well with my city-slicker husband after a few nights into the trip," Nandi recalled, with a smile.

At the end of day four in the bush, Adam drove them to a private tented camp - a *really, really* private, tented camp in Serengeti's central region. Nandi and Mason were the only guests for the night. "We got there, and we were the only tent in the entire camp. It was private as private could be. No guns, no protection… out in the middle of Serengeti somewhere. I planned this entire trip, so truly my husband had no idea what I was getting him into," Nandi explained. After dinner, they crawled into their tent hoping for a good night's rest. "At first, the night seemed very silent, which I guess can be eerie and unusual if you're coming from the burbs. After a little while, we heard lions roaring in the distance, which I thought was thrilling, but when some small animal brushed up against our tent, I suddenly got a hard elbow in the side from Mason yelling, 'what was that?' and 'oh where the bleep have you brought me?' At one point, he starts yelling for the camp staff to come, because in the bush, you're not allowed to leave your tent at night. I swear it was one of the longest nights of my life," Nandi shared with a laugh. Finally, camp staff arrived at their tent armed with a flashlight and past experience dealing with anxious guests and assured Mason that it was likely a porcupine or a Rock Hyrax (think big, overweight prairie dog but with fangs) scurrying around the camp.

The next day, the sleep-deprived pair woke at 4:30 a.m. for a previously scheduled balloon ride over the Serengeti. By the time they returned, Adam devised a plan to ensure Mason wouldn't have another panic attack during the second night at the tented camp which included a little visual reinforcement. Adam arranged for two park rangers — both wielding rifles — to drop by Mason and Nandi's tent to check and see how they were faring. The rangers told the couple that they patrol the camp on foot at night and assured them they were "very safe here, very safe." In some high-end tent camps, guests are given three devices to alert staff of possible danger and are told in what order to use them. First, there's a small walkie-talkie for calling staff. If there's no answer and said beast is rubbing up against the tent walls, use the whistle second. If that doesn't work and help hasn't arrived and the animal is undeterred, then there's the portable air horn fueled by compressed air and, likely, extreme terror.

Adam took a quieter approach. He put his pup tent next to theirs and pulled his safari truck around in the very unlikely event they'd need to make a quick getaway from a predator craving a couple from Columbus. "This really did speak to Adam's resourcefulness. He knew my husband was out of his element and was able to calm his nerves with a couple of creative solutions to what seemed like a serious problem at the time. We all look back and laugh at this now," Nandi said.

The rest of the trip went smoothly. They overnighted at Serena Lodge on the rim of Ngorongoro crater. Nandi said she was able to check off her list of seeing everything she wanted to, including the endangered Black Rhino. On the way to the airport a few days later, Adam pulled the truck off to the side of the road, and Zubeda, who had joined them in Arusha, asked Nandi to get out of the truck. There, Zubeda began wrapping Nandi in beautiful and colorful African clothes and matching head scarf as a departing gift to her. "This was such a special surprise and a dear moment with a newfound friend. I had no idea I'd be sitting down with Adam in my living room in less than a year talking about the possibility of working for Proud African Safaris."

Chapter Fourteen

THE PLAN

While Steve was making plans in the fall of 2008 to go on safari with Adam that coming January, Adam began working feverishly on a business plan for his safari company. It was now time put his ideas down on paper. For his business plan to be taken seriously, he wanted it to be done correctly, professionally and position the company for long-lasting success. He sought advice from an accountant and a business consultant in Arusha who was experienced in the tourism industry. However, professional advice didn't come cheap — the price tag: $500. Knowing that his new business venture would require seed money, he deliberately began saving his client tips over the past few months.

"I'm glad I got direction from these consultants. It was important that I did things the right way to capture the attention of banks and investors. This might be my one chance," Adam said. While developing the plan was a daunting and expensive task, Adam kept reminding himself that he was ready, willing and well prepared to work toward achieving his dream.

He believes three key characteristics gave him the confidence he needed. In his words, those were "mindly, spiritually and skill." As for "mindly," Adam explained "I'd trained my mind to always think bigger than where I currently am. I had a much bigger picture of the company I dreamed about and wanted." Because Adam was a practicing Christian, he knew he was spiritually strong to achieve his dream. "Life is not easy, especially here in Africa. If you don't think positive things, positive things will not happen for you." Lastly, he possessed valuable skills – his skills as a driver guide, people skills, management skills and skills as a wildlife expert.

Adam had to proceed cautiously, and at times secretly, in establishing his business, because if his current employer discovered he was making plans to ultimately become a new competitor in the safari guide space, that would "be a big problem, a very, very big problem. My current job was my only source of income, even though they were hardly giving me any safaris. I needed that money to survive and provide for my family. I had to be smart and balance my time between work and my business plan."

Once completed, the plan was around 22 pages and included business basics like a company introduction and mission statement, loan financing options and an ever-growing list of important startup items: office, laptop, cabinets, office chairs, reservation vouchers, telephones and internet connection. It also included more ambitious and costly items like five new safari trucks, a piece of land on which to build an office, a fenced compound with a large garage for the trucks, supplies and safari tents. Adam admits that "it was an aggressive plan. I didn't think about starting slow. I was worried that starting with a weak breath would be a long struggle and could easily threaten a productive business."

Adam and Steve reunited in January 2009 for a two-week safari trip in the central and southern Serengeti. Adam brought along a copy of the business plan, should their conversation turn from wildlife sightings to life plans. "In talking with Steve on the second trip, I noticed he was carrying Tanzania and the Serengeti positively and deeply in his heart. He loved it so much," Adam said. By now, the two had developed a strong friendship. Steve knew how frustrated Adam had become working for other safari companies. One afternoon, while parked in the Lobo Valley – one of the best places in the northern Serengeti for seeing big cats – Adam shared his dream of owning his own business. "The timing was right, and I believed I began the conversation with something simple, like 'Steve, I don't know how much longer I can do this, working for other people. I have to be my own boss.' I was really surprised when he asked, 'Okay, what do you need to start you own safari business?'"

That's when Adam took the opportunity to tell Steve about the business plan he'd been preparing over the last few months and provided him with an executive summary of its contents. As the game drive continued, they discussed the plan in more detail, and when they got back to the tented camp later that afternoon, Adam gave Steve a hard copy to review. "I was impressed that Adam had the drive and ambition to put together a plan. However, when I read through it in more detail — what with like ten new trucks, the compound, standalone safari tents in the Serengeti — it added up to be like a million-dollar investment, which wasn't going to happen," Steve recalls. Actually, Adam says it was more like

$250,000. Regardless, getting into the safari business can be an expensive undertaking.

After Steve returned to Massachusetts and went through the document more carefully, he called Adam and told him rather bluntly, "Adam, this is what we are going to do. We are going to buy *one* used truck and build a website." Adam said his initial reaction was "not so positive. But on the other-hand, Steve didn't say, 'let's wait for another two years so we can do it.' Since we are rolling and appearing to be moving in the right direction, that was a good thing. I knew my original business plan was a big request, so I started to prepare myself to move forward with a smaller plan." And, he also had to figure out how to leave his current employer, a soon-to-be-rival safari company.

"I really didn't tell them I was resigning the job or tell them that I was leaving because it could have been a threat for me to say, 'I'm leaving to stand on my own and start a business.'" He was afraid his current employer would do practically anything to try and stand in his way of becoming a new competitor. Instead, Adam told his employer he had to take care a family emergency at a clan's village in Ngorongoro and that he would be gone for three weeks. They refused his request, but he left anyway. Shortly thereafter, they attempted to track Adam down, even sent "spies to his home,' according to Zubeda, but Adam had more important work to tend to.

For starters, he decided on a company name: Proud African Safaris. According to Adam, the name, which he often refers to simply as PAS, speaks directly to not only what they offer but also the service they provide to clients. The logo, which Adam initially sketched out on a notepad, features an elephant whose back morphs into an outline of Mt. Kilimanjaro and then into a lion cub. Two acacia trees sprout from the African portion of the Proud African Safaris type.

Adam said this imagery has meaning. "The elephants, being the largest land animal, speak to our strength in the safari field. Mt. Kilimanjaro, the highest mountain in all of Africa, speaks to our uniqueness in providing fantastic safaris to clients. The lion cub and the small acacia trees is our way of showing that although we are small, we are strong, determined and ambitious and ready to grow.

Chapter Fifteen

POLE, POLE

In Swahili, "pole, pole" (pronounced "po-lay, po-lay") means slowly, slowly. Guides on Mt. Kilimanjaro often say this to climbers as a reminder to walk at a slow pace to avoid overexerting themselves at high altitudes. It's also a fairly good description about how life – and people – in Tanzania moves. Snarled traffic moves "pole, pole." Service at restaurants is often "pole, pole." And "pole, pole" was a good description of how safari bookings trickled in the first couple of years. In the spring of 2009, Adam and Steve had an ever-growing list of to-dos. They had to formally register the company name; secure bank accounts in the States, as well as in Tanzania, to facilitate wire transfers; finalize the logo; secure web domain names, locate an office; find a web designer; and last but nowhere near least, get the one thing a company needs to take guests on safaris: a truck.

These days, modern safari trucks are a sight to behold. They're built for unforgiving terrain and wide-eyed foreign tourists eager to soak up nature's splendor. Seeing trucks in the bush makes you want to let out your best Tarzan yell, or attempt to hum the theme song to the short-lived, mid-1960s television show, *Daktari*. Toyota Land Cruiser 4x4s with popup roofs for optimum wildlife-viewing are often the vehicle of choice. They tend to be dark green or khaki in color to blend into the scenery. Most have two fuel tanks, two spare tires, three rows of seats and, in some cases, a small mini-fridge squeezed in the back for chilled waters and better yet, chilled Snickers bars – which was the case when I ventured into the bush. The best place to sit is upfront because you're closer to the guide. Plus, it's less bumpy there than sitting in the back over the rear wheel well.

Adam found a fifteen-year old, dark blue Toyota Land Cruiser in Arusha with 200,000 hard-earned, safari-tested miles for roughly $22,000 USD. It wasn't as nice or reliable as the trucks Adam has today, but he knew he had to start somewhere. "I knew the guy who sold me the truck, so I trusted some of things he told me about it — how it was expertly serviced; how it was in good shape; and that it ran smoothly. I learned later that I probably shouldn't have believed all the things he told me," Adam said. "The suspension was horrible. It was leaf spring rather than coil. It was really horrible. When you hit a hole, you felt it throughout your body. You share part of the impact with the truck." Steve footed the bill for the first truck as capital investment in the company. All they needed were clients. And help.

Even when Adam and Steve were talking business while on safari, Adam was keeping his former co-worker and trusted friend Zubeda apprised of the discussions. Since Adam had worked closely with her before, he knew she would ultimately play a role in Proud African Safaris. "She is very trustworthy and honest. Clients love her. She knew the business; she possessed a good work ethic and a good heart," Adam said.

One day, the two met for coffee near the hectic, open-air market in Tengeru known for its wide selection of used footwear and fresh vegetables. Zubeda had since parted ways with her previous employer, after being fed up with their questionable business practices and, sadly, one too many unwelcome advances from unscrupulous driver guides. She was currently working as a seamstress, barely making enough to make thin ends meet.

At their meeting, Adam recounted his discussions with Steve and shared his vision for setting up the business and the office. More importantly, he spoke with Zubeda about how "to build courage within ourselves. Here, I was asking Zubeda to help me with this new business, and she agreed, even though it would be months before I could pay her a salary. This was also a big step to me. I had to figure out how to adapt to all the new ways of a new business. It was much different than being a driver guide," Adam said. It was no surprise that Zubeda agreed quickly to join the company as Operations Manager. "I knew Adam had this dream. We talked about it a lot. He had this drive to succeed and to be an ambassador for our country. And, he was one of the best driver guides I ever met. I knew in my heart he would do big and important things, and I wanted to be a part of that," Zubeda said.

Adam and Zubeda found office space on Nelson Mandela Road, five miles from Arusha's city center in the spring of 2009. They've been there ever since despite a 300 percent increase in rent over the last ten years – from $50 USD per month to $150 USD. It's located among a hodgepodge of small businesses: a hardware store, banana market, a smattering of darkened doorways claiming to be restaurants, one cosmetic shop and the ubiquitous motorcycle repair shop.

PAS shares the top floor of a simple two-story concrete block structure with a music studio. The office itself is about twice the size of an office elevator. Two small desks take up most of the room. Its cream-colored walls are bare except for a framed 8x10 color photo of the Tanzanian president and a few business certificates. Twice during business hours, a Muslim call to prayer competes with the sound of commerce outside their window.

"For many months, we have a company, we have experience, and we have the big knowledge, but we don't have the clients," Adam said. The two of them would arrive at the office bright and early, fire up the laptop and the intermittent internet and send a flurry of emails to past clients and connections, most of which were in the United States. The majority of the responses were congratulatory and many assured Adam they'd book with PAS if they decided to go on safari again. Some provided additional contact names, and quite a few encouraged Adam visit the States because that's where most of his past clients were from. "That was an interesting and a very smart idea. I was very surprised that almost all of my friends in the States who said, 'Adam, you must come here,' invited me to stay with their families in their homes."

Let that sink in for a second. Yes, people make friends while traveling. If you don't get to know the people, your understanding of the place will be no different than the canned descriptions in travelogues and travel blogs. But it is interesting, and maybe rare, that Adam's past clients, whose interaction with him was limited to a week or so in the bush, formed a special bond where they would, without hesitation, open their hearts, front doors, contact lists and, in some cases their wallets, to a man from a foreign country chasing that boundary-less dream of self-achievement.

According to Jody Yanovich of Atlanta, who has hosted Adam on a number of occasions, "Adam represents the best in humankind. His passion and love for his family, his country, and those people who are in need and the beautiful animals of Tanzania is a quality that each of us strive to achieve. The only driving force in Adam's world is simple: love. For those of us who have had the great fortune of spending any amount of time with Adam, our hearts are drawn to a man whose goals are filled with nothing but the desire to care for his beautiful country and every type of being who lives there."

Chapter Sixteen

GETTING TO AMERICA

International travel is fraught with challenges: flight delays, jet lag, language barriers, in-flight B (make that C-minus) movies and peculiar- looking chicken-n-rice dishes served in aluminum containers the size of a deck of cards. For Adam, it was lack of money, lack of the required travel visa to enter the States and the emotional burden of leaving his family for up to two months. At first, Steve questioned Adam's decision to come to the States because there was no business on the books and no money in the bank, but later agreed it would be good for PAS in the long run.

"I knew in my mind that no matter how many emails I write, I'll continue to get a very good response and good congratulations. I had to take a risk and go meet with past clients and friends in the States." Throughout life, he's experienced first-hand the benefits of networking –from the doctor who helped fuel his passion for science, to the visitors of family's biogas operation, to friends he met on safari who are a continued source of encouragement.

Often, great opportunity lies in who you know. Now, he was more than just a driver guide, but also a businessman, salesman, marketing representative and head cheerleader for his new company. And the best place to drum up business was where his contacts lived: America.

You can't get a tourist visa in Arusha, but you can get a bus to Dar es Salaam that will take you to the U.S. Embassy that issues them. Dar es Salaam is the former capital of Tanzania. That honor now belongs to Dodoma. Getting to Dar e Salaam is a laborious ten-hour bus ride southeast of Arusha. This ever-sprawling, ever-dense, soon-to-be-more-than-just-over-congested megalopolis is the ninth fastest growing city in the world with a current population of just over 4.6 million, according to World Population Review. Its metro population is expected to grow to over five million in the next three years. Some even predict Dar es Salaam will be the second most populated city in the world by 2100, with a whopping 76 million people calling it home. Take present-day Tokyo, Japan, the most populated city in the world; double it, and you have Dar es Salaam in the 22nd Century.

The central bus station in Arusha is chaotic cluster of buses, bundles and bickering passengers. It's especially overwhelming in the morning, and at night, it can be even dangerous. Buses for the day trip to Dar es Salaam typically leave before 7 a.m., and Adam arrived an hour early to navigate the commotion and locate his bus among the many other colorful buses that jockeyed for prime position. With him was his eight year-old son Steven who was on holiday from school.

Their journey to Dar es Salaam took them through sporadic traffic jams, expansive farmlands and small towns humming with activity before arriving just before sundown. "Along the way, I thought about my business and my family, and how this next stage in life was very important. I also practiced many, many times what I'd say during my interview at the embassy," Adam said.

After spending the night in small guest room in the city, Adam and Steven hired an equally small Tuk Tuk to take them to the embassy. Tuk Tuks are those sputtering three-wheeled motorcycle taxis that are popular forms of transportation in southeast Asia. They are named so because earlier models had a distinctive hum when operating – a "tuk-tuk-tuk-tuk."

The U.S. Embassy in Dar es Salaam occupies a well protected 22-acre plot of land. In 1998, the embassy here and the one in Kenya were simultaneously attacked by truck bombs that killed 224 people, including 12 Americans, and wounded more than 4,500. The United States accused Saudi exile, September 11 mastermind Osama bin Laden of orchestrating the bombings.

They arrived at 8 a.m., an hour before the appointment. Adam had all the necessary paperwork in hand: his passport, visa application, an outline of his trip's purpose, a signed declaration saying he'd return to Tanzania, as well as a detailed explanation about the condition of his family and a reassurance that they'd be safe until he returned. "It was so much information, and I didn't know what questions they would ask. You have to be really prepared and have that convincing power when you speak to the embassy person, the one doing the interviewing," Adam explained.

One of the things that Adam remembers vividly about the embassy's waiting room was that no one was smiling. Fellow applicants sat stone-faced, apparently lost in thought, shuffling and reshuffling paper work and occasionally looking up when a number was called. Emotionless embassy workers sat behind thick plexiglass window panes clicking away on computers and dolling out suspicious glances to the morning's applicants.

Adam admits being a nervous while waiting, but all that changed when his number was called. Confidence replaced anxiety. Determination replaced fear. His son whispered four words to him that were punctuated by a gentle nudge to his mid-section that was not only fitting for the moment, but also for the challenge that lied ahead. "Dad, it's your time."

Adam approached one of the windows. A white woman in her late 30s to early 40s, which he assumed was American, was there to decide his fate. Pleasantries were exchanged through dime-sized holes in the plexiglass window. And then, she hit him with a barrage of questions like: "Why are you going to America?" Why do you think you can do this in America and not somewhere else? How long are you going to stay? Where will you be staying? Who will take care of your family? This went on for about ten minutes, with Adam providing detailed, well-rehearsed answers to every question.

Then, the questions stopped abruptly. She flipped through the papers Adam had given her, signed and stamped one of them and said, "come tomorrow and collect your visa." No congratulations. No encouraging smile. Just a DMV-like robotic demand. Both Adam and Steven smiled. One important, potential obstacle was now behind him, but another was ready to take its place.

If you shop airfares online on multiple sites, sign up for fare alerts, keep your fingers crossed and pray for divine intervention for once-in-a-lifetime deals on airfare, you just might find a round trip airfare from JRO to the United States for under $1,000. Adam didn't have a grand sitting around. His base pay at his previous employer was only $50 a month, with most of his income derived from client tips. And, most of that tip money he had in reserve went towards consultation fees for his business plan.

However trite it may sound, it *literally* took a village for Adam to buy round-trip airfare to the States. He contacted friends and family mainly from his tight-knit clan, which in Tanzanian culture tends to rally support for something that could help the common good. With a slight hint of embarrassment in his voice, Adam said "the cash was a big issue. My family, they have nothing really, no business that provides a good income." Adam often uses the word "family" as a general description for "clan," which he sees as family – and in many instances they are. "Some of my family in the village sold a few goats and sheep and gave me the money."

This was 2009, and this was Tanzania, where airfare could be funded in part by the selling of livestock. Some friends in Arusha chipped in a few dollars. A client in the States mailed him $200 cash. Tanzania's clan dynamic and culture appears to support visionaries, financially and emotionally. "My family, believing that this kid is going to do something special and that he is following his dream, it will eventually benefit the whole family," Adam said.

Although Adam had welcomed hundreds of clients from the United States over the years, he never gave too much thought about where cities were located in relation to one other. On occasion, he still thinks Boston is a state. His initial plan was to fly to Phoenix and fly back from Boston two months later. The travel logistics of where, when and how within the States required more planning. Adam found a world atlas in his pile of old school books but had better luck printing off maps from the laptop in his office. "I typed in Google 'United States' and found the maps I needed, printed them and assembled them into a larger map so I could draw where I was going. Looking back, my journey was probably too zig-saggy." His chosen route was to fly to Phoenix, then Salt Lake City, followed by Seattle, Chicago, Columbus and then to Boston, near where Steve lived, and then back to Tanzania. His past clients in those cities picked up the cost of getting him from one place to another. Once again, it took a village.

Adam can't recall the number of times he's been to Kilimanjaro International Airport to pick up clients. Qatar, Air France, KLM, and Ethiopian are just a small list of airlines that service the airport. Adam had flown before — once to South Africa to attend wildlife college there — but this would be the first time he climbed aboard a large, long-haul jet with two-hundred or so fellow passengers.

Adam booked his flight to the states on KLM, a Netherland-based global airline. His flight itinerary took him from Kilimanjaro International (JRO) to Amsterdam (AMS) with a quick stop over in Dar es Salaam. That leg of the trip alone was about eleven hours. Then, from Amsterdam to Phoenix (PHX) was another 13 hours. "I knew it would be a long trip, but I was not nervous but extremely excited. And yes, I was able to sleep some on the plane," Adam recalls.

Some airlines like to announce gate connections upon approach, hoping to provide passengers with advanced intel before deplaning into crowded, and sometimes confusing, international hubs. These announcements can be helpful if you can hear them *and* understand them. Airline manufactures know how to lift a 100-ton hunk of aluminum 30,000 ft. above ground but have yet to design a clear, static-free intercom system. "They were starting to announce things and giving instructions as to what we're supposed to be doing, but the language was too fast and it was so hard to understand," Adam said. A flight attendant tried to put his mind at ease by telling him the information would be repeated, which it was eventually, but he still didn't' know what to do when he got off the plane. So, he simply followed the herd up the jet way into Schiphol International Airport.

Schiphol was the third-busiest airport in Europe in 2009 and has since moved up to third place. Most of the time, people move quickly or sit idly. Adam was the former. He had a connecting flight to make somewhere within its cavernous, albeit ultra-modern terminal. "Everything was so bright and so shiny. I never saw anything like it before, ever. The escalators were amazing. I wanted to stop and gaze around a bit, but I kept telling myself I had to focus on finding my way." Adam was not a big fan of those monstrous computer screens that displayed an ever-changing list of arrivals and departures. He was used to seeing no more than a handful of flights on the screens at JRO. AMS is much different. (In the first quarter of 2018, AMS logged 112,241 arrivals and departures or roughly just over 1,200 a day.) Adam complained that the second he located his flight on the screen, it would change to yet another flight. "Eventually, I found my gate, but I got up every five minutes to look at the screen to see if anything changed," Adam said. "So many planes. So many people."

The flight to PHX was uneventful. He spent time reading, watching movies, sleeping and over-analyzing ways to make his business successful. While the primary goal of his two-month tour of the States was to visit with past clients and drum up new business, he was also interested in finding a U.S.-based sales representative to help facilitate the sales process. "I wanted to get someone from the same culture as America, someone to overcome language barriers, time zones, geographical cultures and all these things. So that when someone is making a decision to go on safari, the response will be quick and efficient, and I won't risk losing the business." He had someone in mind, a past safari client with marketing and advertising experience. And, it was one of his planned stops.

Chapter Seventeen

THE SIX CITY TOUR

Adam selected Phoenix, Arizona to start his American tour, knowing that two other western cities were on his itinerary, Salt Lake City, Utah and Seattle, Washington. In Phoenix, he planned to visit "Old Fritz," whom he first met in August of 2007 during a two-week safari that hit some of Tanzania's most scenic spots: The Serengeti, Ngorongoro and the Grumeti Reserve, a 7,000-square-mile ecosystem about the size of New Jersey that abuts the northern edge of Serengeti's western corridor.

"We fell in love with the guy right away," Fritz explained. "He's a gorgeous man, passionate and a straight-shooter. We have a photograph of him that was taken in the Serengeti. And, there's this lion in the background. And you know, the resemblance was remarkable. Adam has these long dreads that look like a lion's mane, and he's a gentle lion. You can see it in his eyes. He's not fierce but determined, with some feline grace thrown in."

Adam and Fritz kept in touch after their time in the bush. He even tried to get Adam into journalism and photography school in Arizona, thinking it would help his career as a guide, but the enrollment requirements and the ever-present lack of money stood in the way. Nevertheless, Adam reunited with him at Phoenix Sky Harbor International airport, his first formal introduction to the United States.

"People didn't move 'pole, pole' there. They moved fast – the opposite of Tanzania. Overall, I was very impressed with the people. They have different, fantastic attitudes. No one was negative in their minds, Everyone was so friendly and accommodating," Adam recalled.

Fritz drove Adam fifty minutes north to his home outside of Scottsdale. Along the way, they passed many things that most Americans take for granted. Adam was fascinated by neatly designed strip malls influenced by southwestern culture, towering office buildings that, in his words, "looked like they were made of glass," and was amazed that all the roads were paved. Typically, only main thoroughfares in and around Arusha are paved. Back streets and side streets are still mainly dirt with a smattering of gravel. Adam was also a fan of the fall weather in Arizona. He likened it to the dry season in Arusha: warm days, not oppressively hot with cool, clear nights.

At the time, Fritz lived at Desert Mountain which wasn't, and still isn't, your typical American neighborhood. According to the community's smartly designed website, Desert Mountain touts that it's "situated on 8,000 acres in the high Sonoran Desert. Tucked into the rolling hills and dramatic scenery of north Scottsdale, Arizona, Desert Mountain is among the world's finest private golf and recreational communities and is consistently ranked among the country's top private clubs.

Yeah, it's different.

The CEO of Mobile Oil lives there, according to Fritz. And, a modest size four-bedroom home will set you back $900,000 on the low end to upwards of $4 million. "This place where Fritz lived, they call some of the areas there 'villages.' They weren't' the kind of villages I was used to," Adam said with a laugh. They ate dinner at one of the on property clubhouses, where middle-aged to borderline-old men sipped 19th hole libations and shot peculiar glances Adam's way. "Think about it," Fritz explained. You have this guy with his long hair tucked high under his beanie, dark skinned, sunglasses, big smile, strolling among these old white guys in golf shirts and shorts. I don't think they knew what to make of him."

While Adam's visit to Scottsdale was brief, Fritz did arrange three meetings with friends and work colleagues so that Adam could share colorful stories of African safaris and ambitious plans for his company. One meeting was over lunch at the golf club for 15 of Frank's closest friends, followed by less formal and smaller meetings consisting of seven and then five. Adam was armed excitement, thorough knowledge of the bush and a nine-minute long DVD that one of his friends in Arusha had produced. The DVD is a compilation of captivating imagery from Tanzania set to music by the Grammy Award-winning South African male choral group Lady Smith Black Mambazo. This group gained prominence in America when they accompanied Paul Simon on the 1991 hit "Diamonds on the Souls of her Shoes."

On the DVD, there are photos of lions tending cubs or tearing flesh, leopards lounging in tree crooks and pink-bellied hippos lumbering about. There are shots of baby monkeys clinging to dear life and dear moms, while towers of gangly giraffes cast long shadows. Ravenous vultures, their beaks and heads covered in blood, look like something out of a Wes Craven movie. There are grinning guests with floppy hats holding high-priced cameras, porters piling luggage and photos of new friends sharing stories around long wooden tables at luxurious safari camps. Lastly, there are pictures of Maasai in brightly colored robes and well-worn sandals. Young thin boys pose with tall, thin spears while tending underfed goats. It's a simple video production with no voiceover. The music and the montage do the heavy lifting. After nine minutes, the desire to whip out the credit card and book a trip is tempting. Those who listened to Adam's presentation got to take one of the DVDs home – hopefully a gentle reminder that there's more to this world than suburban sprawl, urban crime, headlines, deadlines, tweets and retweets.

"It was my first opportunity to be a salesman for PAS. When you talk to people, you want them to come the next day because it's business, and I had no business. All I could do was hope that they'd consider me sometime," Adam said. Most of Adam's audiences nodded their heads in approval, smiled and politely said that if they one day planned to go on safari, they would consider his services. And so began the slow and difficult process of obtaining clients. Next stop: Salt Lake City, courtesy of Fritz.

The flight from Phoenix to Salt Lake City takes just over an hour, about the same length of time to fly from Arusha to the Serengeti but the jet flies about three times faster. Adam was going to reunite with former clients Mike Wilde and his wife Chris. When they first met in Tanzania, Adam decided to give both of them and their traveling companion semi-official Swahili names. Mike became Baba Kubwa, meaning "great father," because of his tall stature. Adam called Chris Maji Msichana, or "water girl," because she had an affinity for drinking water and making sure everyone in the traveling party was always well hydrated. Their other safari companion was called "Tumbili" because he often ate snacks in small bites, like a foraging monkey.

Adam spent a week with this trio, and they, too, made arrangements for him to present to potential clients at a few pre-scheduled meetings. They also wanted to make sure his visit to Utah was a mix of business, as well as pleasure. Once the presentations were complete, they set off on a four-day road trip to see some of the Southwest's most beautiful natural areas.

First stop was Mirror lake, 1.5 hours east of Salt Lake in the Uinta-Wasatch-Cache National Forest, not too far from the popular ski resort of Park City. It was here that Adam had his first close encounter with snow. On clear days in Arusha, he often saw snow atop Mt. Kilimanjaro but never coughed up the thousands of dollars for the multi-day hike to its 19,341 foot summit, where the air is thin and the snow cap gets thinner as each year passes.

"I had no gloves with me at Mirror Lake. It was freezing up there. I bent down to touch the snow on the ground just with the ends of my fingers at first. It was a fantastic experience, but it was really, really cold – like ice but softer,"

Adam recalls. From there, they set off on a whirlwind National Park tour: Zion, Bryce Canyon, Arches in southern Utah, as well as the northern rim of the Grand Canyon in Arizona. Adam remembers being so connected to nature and inspired by all the things that he saw. "Coming to America, I knew I would get to visit my friends, but seeing some of the natural areas in the States was very special, very different, and something I will never forget," Adam said.

When Adam was planning his trip to America, he learned that there were at least two "Washingtons" – the state and the nation's capital. His preliminary trip itinerary had him heading over to Washington after meeting Nandi in Columbus, Ohio. However, Adam's Washington friends, Leanne and Dave Brown lived in Sammamish, twenty miles east of Seattle. "That's on the other side of your country," Adam confirmed for me when we were discussing his first trip to America. "I am so glad that Leanne told me this. I didn't know."

Most baggage claim areas at major airports have a place set aside for lost luggage. As far as I can tell, none have places for lost entrepreneurs from Tanzania. When Adam arrived at Seattle-Tacoma Airport, or Sea-Tac for short, he gathered his luggage from the carousel and somehow missed the meeting point with Leanne and Dave. The couple spent a good half-hour searching, and because Adam was cellphone-less, they had no way to contact him. The airport's baggage claim is boomerang shaped hall with 12 baggage carousels, 26 doors, and seven bridges leading to a multi-level parking garage. It's not the easiest place to spot misplaced traveler. We were getting a little worried," Leanne explained. "We walked up and down, up and down, and still no sign of Adam. Then we went outside, and there he was, sitting quietly watching all the taxis, buses and cars picking passengers up."

Adam first met the Browns, actually Leanne, her daughter Jennifer and two female friends, in the spring of 2008. This "girls' trip" safari, as Jennifer likes to call it, lasted close to three weeks and hit all of the major wildlife areas west of Arusha. With excitement in her voice, as if she had left the bush just yesterday, Jennifer says, "it was such an amazing trip that's truly hard to explain unless you've been there and experienced it yourself. Words, pictures, videos, stories don't do it justice. They just don't." She must have used the word "love" ten times during our phone interview when describing Adam. "His love of Tanzania, its wildlife, his family and career creates this aura that's infectious, where people who know him, quickly tend love him." She then rattles off a list of his attributes: gracious, humble, intelligent, and passionate. "He's one of my favorite people."

Every once in a while, Adam's humorous side makes a brief but memorable appearance. Jennifer remembered one afternoon on safari when her friends claimed to have spotted lions in the distance and asked Adam if he'd drive over for a closer look. Adam leaned forward, squinted — his eyes zooming with the clarity of a thousand-dollar pair of binoculars — and replied confidently, "nope, those are hyenas." For some reason, the duo challenged Adam's expert assessment, so he made them a simple bet. "I will drive over there now. If they are lions, I will get out of my truck, walk over and pet the lions that you see. If they are hyenas, you have to get out of the truck and pet the hyenas."

The ladies accepted the offer. Adam was right: hyenas. No petting ensued, but a lesson was learned: Trust this man's vision to the point where if he says he sees a flying saucer parked under an acacia tree a mile away, you should get ready for your first alien encounter.

At the time of Adam's visit, Jennifer lived in North Bend, Washington, which rests quietly at the foothills of the Cascade Mountain Range and is a molten-lava-laced stones' throw from the dormant volcano of Mt. Rainer. Forests of large, coniferous trees dominate most of the Cascade Range. Elk, deer, coyote, eagles, hawks are a few of the mammals that call it home. Jen took Adam on a game drive around North Bend hoping to catch a glimpse, or a photo or two, of the wildlife near her home. "Adam was infatuated with all the towering trees and greenery, which is something that he doesn't get to see back home," Jennifer recalled. They didn't have much luck during their drive, only seeing a couple of deer. Elk remained elusive. Birds flittered. The first picture Adam took with his new camera was that of elk poop in her front yard. "That made me laugh so hard because that is true Adam. He's a driver guide and appreciates stuff like that, but a picture of poop? Really?"

Adam calls the Browns "a big, big family." It was they who sympathized with him over ongoing frustrations with management practices of safari owners and encouraged him to start his own business. They were also the ones who paid for him to attend the Limpopo field Academy in South Africa, much to the angst of his current employer. Now, he was with them again, and they were anxious to help him grow his business. Aside from arranging meetings with travel agents, the Browns and another former client called David who surprisingly lived only a mile away, coordinated what they referred to as a "introduction party." David even took out an ad in a local paper, inviting readers to attend the function at his home. In all, roughly 30 people showed up, and Adam gave a brief presentation and worked the crowd. Jennifer remembers how gracious and approachable Adam was, never coming across as a pushy salesman. Evidently, it worked. Adam said nine photographers from the Seattle area booked a safari with PAS less than six months later. "Advertising is important, but it's expensive," Adam said. "Going to America and seeing friends and then meeting their friends is good. It's something I should do every other year at least, but that also costs money but it's been successful."

After Seattle, Adam then made a quick stop in Chicago to visit a couple, Emily and Robert, who honeymooned in the Serengeti in 2003. Adam aptly described Chicago in three words: big, overwhelming and cold. While there, he gave a presentation to 10-15 employees at a computer company. As was the case with presentations and talks in other cities, people were noncommittal. "Many people say, 'I will put this on my bucket list,' or 'I have friends who might be interested in this trip,'" Adam said. Always the optimist, he didn't interpret these responses as people just trying to be nice, but rather said "these kind of things give you hope and inspires me. Maybe they will come. Maybe not. I hope they will."

Come early November, Adam made his way to Columbus, Ohio to visit with Nandi, Mason and forty of their closest friends. Because Nandi's background was in advertising and marketing, she planned a "new business presentation" one night in their home. Invitations were sent, appetizers were served, maps of Africa, Tanzania, Ngorongoro and the Serengeti adorned her walls, photos of their past trip rotated on the big screen television in their living room, and Adam gave a short presentation about being a driver guide and, now, a business owner. The rest of the time, he mingled. "I really liked just speaking with the many people one-on-one at Nandi's house. It was less formal, and it was a good way to meet and connect with their friends," Adam remembered. Plus, the way she presented and coordinated the event, I could tell she would be a good sales person."

A day or two later, while sitting in the loft area of their home, Adam asked if Nandi planned to return to work since giving birth to a baby girl six months prior. She knew juggling a new home life with returning to old ad agency life was not what she wanted to do. Lucky for her, Adam presented an option that would allow her to work part- time from home. There was no formal job description other than "to help with sales," and there was no pay yet because there were no clients. Nandi took a second to think about it, shifted the baby from one side of her lap to another and answered, "sure, why not? It sounds like fun."

Nandi felt like this was a new and different opportunity to help get something up and running. She likened it to launching a new client brand in her pre-mom days as an advertising account person. "I knew it would be commission-based, so it would be whatever I made of it. Actually, I thought it was going to be a short-term gig and that I'd help until they got the business off the ground. Little did I realize how involved and passionate I'd be about my newfound purpose and how close to my friends and family at PAS I would become."

That night, as Adam, Nandi, and Mason sat around the dinner table, Adam turned to Mason and asked permission for Nandi to join PAS. "Talk about a culturally different way to approach things," Nandi said. "I recall the feeling of my face flushing red and my heart coming up into my mouth. I looked at Mason, and he had a slight grin on his face, knowing that Adam's question sounded like he was asking for my hand in marriage or something. Needless to say, I was quite surprised, but Mason handled it well with a simple 'my brother, I think it would be a great idea for Nandi to work with you. We love the people, and we love the country.'"

Nandi knew that in order to sell safaris, she needed more education about Tanzania and the safari industry in general. So, after dinner, dishes were cleared, Adam placed a large map on the table and started talking about the different regions of his country "Selling the excitement piece would be the easy part, because people want to visualize themselves on safari. In the advertising business, we were storytellers. We sell with words and pictures. It would be the same in selling safaris, only my tools would be that much stronger. Think of the exciting stories and pictures I could share with potential clients. How hard could that be?"

Over the next two days, Adam gave Nandi a crash course in the safari businesses. Topics included wildlife and migration patterns, natural areas, downtown Arusha and the all-important location, amenities, and service history of the safari lodges that dot the area. Often, a nice gin and tonic served with a smile at high-end tented lodge is the perfect way to end a game drive in the bush.

Adam knew that he made the right decision in bringing Nandi on board. "She is a smart person, very friendly and a quick learner. I was so happy to have her help with sales and help grow the business. And, I told her she will not be alone. Anything that a client asks, Zubeda and I will be there to help." Adam looked forward to flying to Boston and share the news with Steve who lived in nearby Marblehead.

Marblehead, Massachusetts is a quintessential New England seaside town filled with colonial era homes, quaint inns and restaurants, and a harbor filled with sail boats, their masts adding exclamation points to an already stunning view. And around Thanksgiving, it can get quite cold especially for someone like Adam. Steve remembers that when Adam arrived in Boston, "he had this outfit that looked like what a skin diver would wear. It was some neoprene-looking thing on the top and bottom to protect him from the cold." While there, Adam declined repeated invites for a walk in the snow and chose rather to sit in Steve's front room, which faced south, wrapped in a blanket, drinking cup after cup of coffee. "I think he was there for a week and went through a pound of coffee and a pound of sugar," Steve said.

The pair eventually got down to talking business. Adam told him about the contacts he made and the presentations he gave during his trip, but none had resulted in any confirmed bookings. In his usual rapid-fire delivery, Steve said to Adam, "I told him we need to get someone to help with sales. I'm not good at sales, and I'm not going to talk to people all day. And, I'm not going to put together these itineraries, because I'm too busy doing other stuff, alright? I remember Adam telling me 'Steve, I've got this perfect person. Her name is Nandi, and she came on safari with me with her husband. She just had a baby, so she's not working anymore and is staying home.' So I said, Adam that sounds perfect.'"

Steve was happy with Adam's choice, as long as she wasn't asking for a lot of money – because they didn't have any yet. They wanted to be sure that she was willing to grow with them and feel like she was a part of the business. Steve knew her background in advertising and marketing would be very valuable, but she was coming on board as head of sales, yet had never sold a safari before. Sure, she had been on a trip once, and Adam gave her two-day crash course about Tanzanian safaris, but there was still a lot to learn.

"So, I said to Adam, 'let's get her on the phone and see how it goes,'" Steve recalls. "The call went great; she's very smart and excited about this new position. We're on the phone, and she says 'Steve, what do I tell people? What do I tell people?' So, I just said, you just tell'em, you got the best safari guide in Africa. You just tell'em we going to make the best trip you ever had. Tell'em you got Adam.'"

EPILOUGE

The first few years of most business ventures are characterized by a series of growing pangs, achievements and setbacks, and PAS was no exception. Business trickled in. "2009 probably wasn't the best time to start a business," Adam said. "You had the recession in the States and tourism to Tanzania suffered. But it was my time, and we all had to do our best."

Steve assumed the responsibility of a CFO of sorts, handling the logistics of setting up bank accounts, wiring money, and keeping a close eye on the profit and loss sheet (more loss, than profit at first).

Nandi, who was used to the quick turnaround, deadline-driven, client- demanding, fast-paced advertising world admitted that she had to "take it down a notch. Tanzanian culture has little concept of that pace, and things moved more slowly, which took getting used to." She helped prospective and current clients understand that there may be times when requests for things like additional itinerary options may not be fulfilled the same day. "It was a matter of finding that balance between two culturally different countries, where slow pace versus fast pace is just one of the many contrasting practices. And that's why having a U.S.-based sales person was a good idea.

She later became more involved in the development of marketing strategies, advertising, collateral materials and the website, so when the time came when PAS was in desperate need of a new truck, she approached Steve and Adam with the offer to purchase one as a way of buying her way into becoming a business partner. "By then, it was much more than a job to me. I was passionate about what I was doing and wanted to help this company grow."

Zubeda continued to do what she does best: being that ever personable, ever optimistic, smiling face that meets and greets clients when they arrive in Tanzania. She manages the office, coordinates the booking of lodges and tours and continues to look out for her dear friend Adam –all while attending to a young family. She also took on the daunting task of helping young Tanzanian women and girls navigate the treacherous route to womanhood. According to *The Citizen*, a Tanzanian newspaper, sixty percent of women in this country experience domestic abuse. Then, there's that crippling practice that if students don't pass a test to get into secondary school (high school here in the States), they are left to find a job in a less-than-job-rich county where the unemployment rate by some accounts hovers around 10 percent — and the reporting of said unemployment rate is questionable. Combine that with the antiquated tradition of fathers deciding to sell their teenage daughters into prearranged marriages in exchange for cattle, and the job prospects for young women is grim, to say the least.

Seeing a need, Zubeda and Adam started a nonprofit called Skilled Hands Tanzania, whose mission is teaching women the sewing trade. Zubeda takes in young women from Arusha and surrounding villages, often three or four at a time, into her home and teaches them to sew. Every few weeks, she collects discarded scraps of cloth, many of which are mere strips, from various shops in Arusha. When Zubeda dumps out a canvas bag full of the week's haul, out pours a fettuccine of colorful fabric that will be transformed into aprons, oven mitts, earrings and handbags. Zubeda and the girls then sell these up-cycled items at local markets to raise enough money to buy a sewing machine for a girl to take back to her village and start her own business as a seamstress. (A portion of the proceeds from this book are going to Skilled Hands Tanzania.)

Adam finally became more than just a driver guide but a business owner, and ambassador for his country with countless friends throughout the world. But like any new business owner, he's restless. He's always wanting to do more and be more, as he's done his entire life. He still wants ten trucks, an office compound and safari lodges. "The first couple of years of the company, I wanted to grow fast, but the resources were not there yet. Steve kept giving me a heart. He kept saying to me, 'let's grow slowly and learn how to do things the right way.' We have been growing slowly, one safari at a time. It took time and sacrifice, but over the ten years, I've made so many friends and have helped them experience so many wonderful things. It brings me such joy…life is good. I'm proud we're making good progress. Really proud."

DRIVE

Greg Ward

ABOUT THE AUTHOR

Greg Ward has over twenty-five years' experience in tourism marketing and has been an avid traveler since first piling in his parent's Winnebago motorhome as a child. His articles have appeared in *The Virginian Pilot, The Virginia Beach Beacon, Hampton Roads Business Weekly,* and familytravels.com. This is his first book. He currently lives in Virginia Beach, Virginia with his wife Debb.

Made in the USA
Monee, IL
25 January 2021

58595254R00080